BEFORE GRANDPA WAS THIRTEEN

Stories I told my Grandchildren

*Grandpa John Morris Benson with new watch
and "bibs" for 12th birthday. Van Hook, ND,
and family outhouse in background.*

BEFORE GRANDPA WAS THIRTEEN

Stories I told my Grandchildren

John Morris
Benson

Some of the stories previously appeared in the author's blog. These short stories about when I was young are true or nearly true. Some have been modified to protect the guilty[1], or embellished a little to fill in details that may have or could have been.

ISBN: 13-978-1-7326129-6-9

PUBLISHED BY: Benson Tech Write

Printed in the United States of America

Cover design by John Morris Benson

Cover photograph from Pixabay sources
Included photographs from family collections
Author photograph by Shirley Benson

---

[1] Me

Before Grandpa was Thirteen
is dedicated to my grandchildren
Sarah, Calin, Leslie, Patrick, Ryan, Isaac, Lynn,
and
great-grandchildren Theo and Emma-Grace

Children's children are a crown to the aged,
and parents are the pride of their children.
Proverbs 17:6

Buster Bunny Note

The Buster Bunny stories I made up, told to my grandchildren, and included in this work are mine; subsequently, I discovered at least two other fictional rabbits named Buster Bunny. One was a character in Standard Comics, and another appears in the Tiny Toon Adventures copyrighted by Warner Bros. However, just as there is more than one John Benson, there is more than one Buster Bunny.

All of my Buster Bunny stories start, "Now, Buster Bunny was not a regular rabbit; he lived in a city." The three older granddaughters almost immediately memorized the opening lines and were able to recall and recite most of the first paragraph some twenty years after not hearing it.

Several years ago, the granddaughters encouraged me to 'write up' the stories so they could have copies. Needless to say, I could not remember all of the BB stories I told off the cuff. I did however 'write up' the few I had told several times with minor variations.

- 0 -
Foreword

S everal years ago, one grandkid, Sarah I think, said, "I've heard that one at least once Grandpa, but you should write it down in case you or one of us forgets what you said." More recently, Calin said that I should get this published.

Actual memories of things that happened 'way-back' in the 1940s are difficult for me to recall with any measure of precision. However, telling it how it must have been or how it probably was or as I really did remember was easy. And, many stories were just extended answers to questions about 'what did you do when?' One example was telling how I learned to swim.

Memory triggers – pictures of places, people, and events were usually sent to others and copies were rarely saved. And as you'll read, my parents didn't usually stay in one place long enough to pick up processed photographs after turning in the film. (Not that I remember if they did or not.)

This generation will have selfies and personal video files from which to write their stories. However, they will still have to take the time to collect and arrange their memories.

Parts of my stories might be thoroughly debunked by questioning of witnesses if they could be found or are willing to testify against themselves or me.

The exact sequences of events may also be somewhat out of order, but if anyone over 70 at this writing who was there and has a better memory than I, you will know. If you weren't there, what difference does it make? After all, these are just my stories, not testimony under oath in court or in a congressional hearing. And, if the version of a story sounds different from how you heard it before, refer to the previous sentence.

I've called my mother by the name my children and grandchildren knew her – Grandma Marvel. Grandma Benson refers to my paternal grandmother and Grandmother Larson was my mother's mother. Aunt Lyla, Uncle Elmo and Uncle Kermit were Grandma Marvel's siblings.

Grandma, my wife, isn't mentioned in any of the stories, nor are our children. The title should tell you so.

My children know my siblings as uncle or aunt, grandchildren also know them as such, so to fit how I told the stories orally that's how they are referred to in this work.

Have fun reading.

---

[2] Kermit isn't in any of the stories. I don't remember meeting him until after I was thirteen.

- 1 -
Too Early to Remember

I remember only what I've been told about Sanish, North Dakota, where I was born. Grandma Marvel was born on the Ft. Berthold Indian Reservation south of Sanish, east of the Missouri River in 1916. She seldom said much about when she was young, even when I asked.[3] My father was born in Charlson, ND, in 1914 and his widowed mother settled in Sanish when he was about nine. I've heard very

Spring 1937 – John Morris Benson in Sanish

---

[3] For many years, I understood that Grandma Marvel was the first non-Indian girl born on the reservation where her parents bought land designated as open by federal government action. Her being 'first' is not likely because the reservation was occupied by several small towns of mostly non-Indian people.

few stories about when my father was young, and I don't remember his telling any.

Dr. Blatherwick Sr. delivered me at home shortly after midnight on Monday, October 19, 1936, his birthday. I was named John after my father and was told that my middle name Morris was for Morris Samuelson a friend of his.

Uncle Lowell was born in Sanish when I was about eighteen months old. Uncle David was born there at the end of December in 1940.

Sanish back yards in 1937

Grandma Benson operated the Bell Telephone Company switchboard and lived in a room or two in the back of the office. Grandma Benson didn't tell many stories and children did not – DID NOT – ask questions in Grandma Benson's home.

I don't know where my Uncle Gilbert Pederson, Grandma Benson's brother, lived but it seems he was usually sitting in a rocking chair at the telephone office smoking a cigar. Grandma Marvel said she could tell if he was there before she saw him because of the cigar smell. He worked as a clerk in the Sanish hardware store and wore striped dress shirts with arm garters. Grandma Marvel said it was him who took me for my first haircut.

Grandmother Josine and Uncle Gilbert
***

Grandpa Larson (Louis L) and Grandma Emma moved from their farm near Sanish to a new farm near Brandon, Minnesota, when I was a baby. [1936 had one of the longest and coldest winters and one of the hottest summers on record. History says farming in ND was usually tough in those days, but even the hardiest of crops didn't grow that year.]

Grandma Marvel said that we visited her parents in Minnesota before my brother Uncle Lowell was born. The picture of me and the chickens was taken at their farm. Aunt Lyla, Grandma Marvel's younger sister, told me that she got in trouble when I threw eggs out the pantry window when she was supposed to be watching me.

I have no memory of Grandpa and Grandma Larson until we moved to Minnesota when I was twelve. And, I don't remember hearing stories about their younger days.

Grandma Marvel's brothers Kermit and Elmo no longer lived at the farm (or so I was told).

I believe we left Sanish in 1941 when I was still four.

- 2 -

Lowell and the Big Worm

Grandma Marvel told several variations of this story over the years. I've tried to meld as many variations as I can remember, but as I said before about memory, …

I was nearly four years old and Uncle Lowell was just over two in the late summer of 1940. Grandma Marvel, (pregnant with Uncle David) Uncle Lowell, and I lived in a log cabin across the Missouri River from Sanish, ND[4]. The inside wall that separated the kitchen area from the sleeping area was constructed of rough-cut boards. Rough boards over the dirt floor in the kitchen and eating room were covered in places with patches of linoleum. The sink below the only window in that room drained into a five-gallon bucket. A long curtain was hung in the door size opening between the rooms. The sleeping room had a window, but it was boarded over with small open spaces to let in light but keep small animals out. It had a hooked rug on the dirt floor.

There was no electricity. Water for drinking, washing up, bathing and watering the garden came from the river just over 100 yards away. The water was muddy, so it had to

---

[4] I do know why, but that's not part of these stories.

settle in the bucket before we could skim off the top for drinking or cooking.

The outhouse was about 100 feet farther away from the river than the cabin in a sparse grove of cottonwood trees. In one sense, that made us no worse off than people in Sanish. Indoor plumbing during that time was rare even in small rural North Dakota towns.

People gave Grandma Marvel corn, green beans, peas and beets which she canned if there was too much to eat in a few days. There was a kerosene stove in the cabin but all except the beans were often eaten without being cooked. Because of the possibility of botulism, green beans were always boiled for twenty minutes. There was little waste. The skins from the vegetables were buried along the edge of her small garden as compost. Even gray water from the kitchen drain wasn't wasted; it was used to wash the outhouse bench.

Any bone-in meat, a rare treat for Grandma Marvel, was eaten to the gristle and the left-over bone was used for soup. Table scraps and used soup bones went to our pet wirehair terrier named Jiggs.

Grandma Marvel was starting lunch and told me to find Lowell. He was always running off and I'm sure she feared that he would go down by the river and stumble into the fast-moving current. I found him standing by the garden as if frozen but with tears running down his face. I soon found out why he was motionless and crying silently.

Jiggs was guarding him from a large snake coiled a few feet in front of him. I thought it was just a giant night crawler like those I had seen Grandma Marvel put on a hook and cast into the river.

He remained motionless and I ran to the cabin to tell her that he was being scared by a big worm. She grabbed a garden hoe from outside the cabin door and ran to the garden. Lowell and I watched as she chopped the snake into bite size pieces. Jiggs might have eaten them; Grandma Marvel said we didn't, but some people did eat snake meat.

I never knew for sure if it was a rattlesnake or a bull snake until I was a teenager when Grandma Marvel filled in some of the details. It was a bull snake and they were not aggressive, but she didn't know until her first chop removed its head.

A headless snake of any kind is harmless.

- 3 -
Phil and Midge

After we moved to Alexandria, MN, in 1950. I had a walking paper route but wanted a bicycle so I could get a second route. The only one I found that I could afford with my paper route savings was a very much used, English made, Elgin skip-tooth-chain bicycle at a secondhand store. I knew the tires were poor but when I pumped them up at a service station, the tubes wouldn't hold air. I tried to buy tires and tubes but none of the hardware stores in town had them because it was an import from England.

OK – OK, you're probably wondering what this has to do with before I was 13. Be patient, I'll get there.

I remembered that Clyde Newstrom who owned a hobby shop had catalogs for nearly everything. He ordered tires and tubes for me from a Minneapolis bike dealer and I pushed the bike home on its rims.

Grandma Marvel told me that the 'skinny wheel' bike reminded her of meeting a newlywed couple named Phil and Midge at the Yellowstone River campground where the Yellowstone flows into the Missouri River just west of Watford City, ND. They were riding bicycles from Chicago to the west coast on their honeymoon.

Told you so!

She said that it was dusk when they arrived at the campground on imported touring bicycles. In the morning, they were gone, and their campfire pit was still warm but damp from being doused with water. We passed them on the road later in the day.

They arrived before dark at the campground along a river where we had stopped for the night. Grandma Marvel said that they had only dried food in their bicycle saddle bags, so she shared our ground beef and potato stew with them.

The next morning, they left the campground before we were up, and again, we passed them on the road during the day, and we met again at a campground near Billings, MT.

They were gone the next morning and we never saw them again. I learned later that they had plans to ride south into Wyoming before heading west to California. We went to Butte.

---

[5] In 2006, Ryan went with us on a road trip to Virginia. On the way back we stopped at a rest area in Wyoming. While there, we talked to newlyweds traveling by bicycle to Oregon. In 2010 while traveling with Sarah and Eli, we met another couple riding from Boston to Oregon. Ironically, it was at the same rest stop.

Both were reminders of the differences in their bikes, my Elgin, and those that Phil and Midge rode. I guess every bicycle has a story.

Buster Bunny and the Loud Music

Now, Buster Bunny was not a regular rabbit; he lived in a city. Buster had a mother Mommy, a father Daddy, an older sister Bonnie, an older brother Bobby, a younger sister Betty, and an even younger brother Baby. None of these bunnies were regular rabbits. They all lived in a city called Taleton. Most of the time, Buster was a nice kind and quiet boy bunny, but he could get into mischief with very little effort.

Buster was given a new tape player for his birthday. Buster even got some tapes from a friend. Buster liked listening to all kinds of tapes.

He even had some tapes of his family just talking. Many of those were from a time when Buster was just a baby and started with Daddy saying, "Buster, say Mama."

One started with Mommy saying, "I don't like talking on these things. Well, OK. Say Dada, Buster."

One day the sun was shining, but it was not too hot outside so Buster asked his mother, "May I take my tape player and some tapes outside?"

"Yes," she said, "but be sure you do not get sand or dirt in the player or tapes because they may not work right after that."

Buster replied, "OK Mother. I will be careful."

He went out and sat near Neighbor's fence. Buster put a music tape in the player and pressed the play button. His brother Bobby was playing with some toys on the other side of the yard.

Bobby shouted, "Buster, will you turn up the sound so I can hear the music too?"

"Yes." Buster shouted back. He turned up the volume, so the music was loud enough for his brother to hear at the other side of the yard.

His mother was running the vacuum cleaner inside, so she did not hear how loud the music was.

Another time she had told Buster and Bobby that Neighbor worked at night and needed to sleep during the day. She told them that they should play music quietly and not shout too loudly when they were in the yard during the week. It was OK, of course, to make reasonable noise on the Saturday or Sunday afternoons but never late at night because other neighbors would be sleeping.

Buster went to the other side of the yard to play with his brother and the music did not seem too loud for them. He and Bobby were playing with some toy trucks and making engine noises when Mommy came into the yard saying, "What are you two doing? Neighbor just called me and said you had the music on so loud it woke him up."

"It's not loud over here, Mommy." Buster said.

Mommy said, "Go get your tape player from the other side of the yard, shut it off, and bring it here."

Buster did what his mother told him because that was what he usually did. When he brought the tape player to where his mother was, she said, "Now turn it back on."

Buster did and he realized that the music was very loud. He said, "I will apologize to Neighbor and I will remember that just because it does not seem loud to me, it might be too loud for someone else."

And, that ends another story about Buster Bunny, who was not a regular rabbit because he lived in a City.

– 4 –
Butte, MT

The first place I remember after North Dakota is Butte, Montana. I was four and a half years old in the summer of 1941. I have no idea why or how long we were there. We lived in the daylight basement of a house on a hillside in town. The hill was so steep that when we went out the door, we could see only the eve of the roof on the next house.

The kitchen had a green enamel kerosene stove and oven like the one in the log cabin on the river, but it was newer. The apartment had a real floor but just like the cabin, the kitchen was also the living room. We three brothers shared one of the two bedrooms.

We still had our dog Jiggs; he followed me around whenever I explored. And explore I did. I seldom went anywhere that I couldn't see where we lived. However, one morning I wandered farther away than usual and had no idea where I was. As usual, Jiggs was with me.

I didn't have a watch but had a general idea of the time when I saw a clock. I was told by Grandma Marvel that I could count and understood some number concepts by the time I was three. I knew it was time for lunch when the bells on the clock tower in the center of town rang 12 times. And

17

when the bell sounded six times I'd better be on the back stoop or inside.

When I heard the 12th gong during one of my wandering days, I started home without being sure which way to go. Without knowing it, I did a grid search. I just went up one street to the top end of town and down the next to the bottom. Had I known better, I would have taken the horizontal streets instead of the uphill and downhill streets. I eventually found the place where we lived.

Me, David, and Lowell the spring
before we left Sanish for Montana

I should have followed Jiggs, but every time he left me, I thought he was running away. Later I realized he knew the way home but would not abandon me in my errorness (is that a word?). Even when I was young, I often took the hard way first.

- 5 -
Jiggs

O ur white, wirehair terrier Jiggs traveled with us from North Dakota to Butte, MT, during the late summer of 1941. Jiggs was less likely to wander off than me or my younger brother Lowell. But, when we left Butte for parts west, Jiggs wasn't with us. Grandma Marvel told me that we were all sad, but we couldn't wait for him to show up. She assured us that he was so cute and gentle natured that someone would give him a good home.

It was fruit and berry harvest time (I think), so we stopped at Post Falls, ID. I never saw Jiggs there and just assumed he was gone forever. We lived in a cabin next to another family with more kids than ours. Having lunch with them one day was my first experience with a lard sandwich and I missed Jiggs when they fed table scraps to their dog.

Jiggs showed up on a back road near Spokane, WA, when we were there to pick apples after being in Post Falls. Jiggs was with us when I got to help pick potatoes in the Kittitas Valley.

Years later Grandma Marvel showed a picture of a boy on a spotted pony. She said his family name was Knolls and they didn't like Jiggs – he barked at their pony.

Sometime later we moved to Kalama and lived in one of the three cabins behind a gas station on a road now known as Old Pacific Highway. We met a family there with a son they called Bucky. Buck Jr. was just a little older than me and had a dog named Nickel.[6]

An ice cream cone cost a nickel and one Washington State tax token. Bucky said that we should change Jiggs's name to Token so we could trade the dogs for an ice cream cone.

Jiggs, Lowell and me in Sanish.

I turned six in Kalama but couldn't start school with Bucky because the cut-off date for enrollment was October 15. They wouldn't waive the 4-day difference.

Aunt Connie was born in Longview when we lived in Kalama. And That's where Uncle David got run over by the babysitter's boyfriend.

---

[6] Many years later, when I was teaching in Kelso, Washington, I had Bucky's son (called Buck III) in class for a short period of time, but not long enough to find more about his father.

We must have been in Kelso when Pearl Harbor was bombed. Grandma Marvel said we were on a picnic – seems to be an odd event for December 7th, but Washington weather wouldn't always keep someone from doing that. I was told that we didn't find out until the radio was turned on that evening.

I don't know what happened to Jiggs, and I don't remember Grandma Marvel saying what may have happened to him, but he wasn't with us when we were in Texas to harvest cotton.

- 6 -

Cotton and Watermelon

The first time we were in Texas was in October just before I turned seven, I think, but memory is ... well you know. Gosh! Maybe I was only six because I don't remember Aunt Beth being there. She was born in July of '43. However, and there's nearly always a however when memory is fading, I really do remember the melon part of the story.

Grandma Marvel said that we went there to pick cotton after my parents helped harvest the last of the walnut crop in California but before we went to Los Angeles. Living in a cotton field campground wasn't like orchard camps where finding tree shade was easy. It was hot, dry and the only shade was under the side-less pole barn where the cotton was pressed into bales. The canvas lean-to alongside our car gave relief from the sun but not the heat.

Like other migrant camps, there were kids with their field working parents. Those of us old enough picked along with the adults. The picking bag had a strap to go over the shoulder and pickers dragged it between the rows. Kids and small women were given smaller bags, but the process was the same as for men. The spiny bolls were plucked from the bush and shoved into the bag.

Grandma Marvel was small, but she could drag a man size bag. When a bag was full or as heavy as one could pull, it was dragged to the supervisor, weighed and then emptied. My back hurt and, like other workers, at the end of a day in the field my hands were cut from the sharp edges on the bolls.

One evening a boy in the camp gave me my first taste of watermelon. A day or so later, he asked if I wanted to go with him just before dark to get another melon. I'm sure that I thought we would be going to a store, but I was wrong. He came to our campsite just as the sun was down, but the light hadn't faded away. We walked on a dirt road to a watermelon field a good distance from where we had picked cotton.

I thought nothing of going into the field because we often picked up culls to eat in the orchards. In the field, he showed me how to tap on a melon to tell if it was ripe.

We were several yards away from the fence with our 'free' melons when I heard a yell. He dropped the melon he was carrying and ran. I followed. I heard a gun blast and dropped my melon.

I realized watermelons in a field were not like apple or pear culls for free picking.

Buster Bunny and Neighbor's Garden

ow, Buster Bunny was not a regular rabbit; he lived in a city. Buster had a mother Mommy, a father Daddy, an older sister Bonnie, an older brother Bobby, a younger sister Betty, and an even younger brother Baby. None of these bunnies were regular rabbits. They all lived in a city called Taleton. Most of the time, Buster was a nice kind and quiet boy bunny, but he could get into mischief with very little effort.

One day Buster was outside by himself. All of his brothers and sisters were inside playing. Buster did not want to be inside because he thought the weather was too nice. Buster played with his toys, and then just walked around his yard for a while. As he was walking, he saw the fresh carrot tops in Neighbor's garden.

Now, his mother had taught him to stay out of other people's property, but that day the temptation was just too great. First, he looked all around to see if anyone was watching him. Then he dug a little hole under the fence with his sharp toenails. Buster looked again to see if anyone was looking then quickly crawled under the fence into his neighbor's garden. That was not like Buster at all. Most of the time he was a nice, kind and quiet boy bunny.

Mommy Bunny called for everyone in to get cleaned up for supper, but because Buster was outside, he did not hear his mother call. She thought Buster was inside with the rest of the bunnies.

Buster looked around but did not see Neighbor watching him from the back steps of his garden shed.

Bunny family's neighbor was not a mean man, but he had spent a very long time planting his garden so there would be vegetables for his family's supper. When he saw Buster crawl under the fence, he was not angry, but just disappointed because the Bunny family had always been good neighbors.

At first Neighbor thought that Buster was just looking at the plants. When Buster started to take a bite out of a carrot top, the neighbor yelled in a deep, loud voice, "Get out of my garden you pesky rabbit." In fact, he yelled so loudly that Buster's mother heard him from inside the Bunny's house.

Buster scooted through the opening he had made and was already running towards his house when he heard his mother call, "Buster! Come here right now!"

Buster knew he had done something wrong, but he pretended otherwise as he stood in front of her and said, "I'm coming in for dinner now Mother. Is that what you want me for?"

She said, "Buster, have you been in Neighbor's garden?"

Buster Bunny knew it was wrong to lie so he said, "Yes mother. I guess I was too tempted to think right. I know I was wrong, and I will ask Neighbor to forgive me."

Neighbor did forgive Buster and Buster learned that even if he is tempted to do something wrong, he should resist the temptation and do only what he knows is right.

And, that ends another story about Buster Bunny, who was not a regular rabbit because he lived in a City.

- 7 -
Los Angeles

When my father worked in a Los Angeles, California, shipyard I really was seven. Our apartment was just a few blocks away from LA's famous Figueroa Street. It was my first close experience with cultures, races and spaces different from my North Dakota roots and the orchard camps. There were Mexicans in the fruit picking crews. I don't remember seeing Blacks (they were called Negros then) until we were picking cotton but like with the Mexicans where they spent their nights was separated from us.

All of the brick buildings on the street where we lived in LA looked the same from the street, but instead of by campsites, people were separated by buildings. Our corner apartment building had only Whites. Mexicans lived in the building next to us and Chinese lived in the next one.

The man who picked up my father for work in the mornings came from the Chinese apartments. He and

---

[7] I told my mother in the 1980s that I was going to a vocational teacher conference at the Los Angeles Convention Center and that I would be staying in a Hotel on Figueroa St. She asked me to see if the Pantry Café was still on Figueroa. It was only a few blocks from where we lived in 1943. I ate there several times while at the convention. At this writing, the café that opened in 1924 is still in business at the same location.

another man from his building would park in front of our second story apartment and he would shout, "Bean-soon, Bean-soon, time to work."

I'm not sure if the Chinese man had children because I don't remember hanging out with any.

One day I was with a Mexican boy at his apartment when his grandfather asked me if I wanted some tamale caliente. The boy translated his question. I just thought it was a Mexican word for hot oatmeal because that was what the children were eating.

I was too embarrassed to admit that I didn't know what he was talking about and took the tamale. He showed me how to peel back the corn husk wrapping and take a bite. My friend took a nibble of his and continued eating. I took a large bite.

It was the hottest thing I had ever eaten in my life. The grandfather couldn't help seeing my surprise at the heat of it after I started chewing. He laughed. I did the tough boy thing and finished it.

Every time I went there after that, he asked me if I wanted tamale caliente. Then he would laugh. I learned very quickly how to say, "No thanks," in Spanish. (I like tamales now – even the hot ones.)

Another time when I was with the same boy, some older boys asked us if we wanted to be in their club. We took the invitation; however, neither of us knew there would be conditions. The one who seemed to be their leader told us that one of the things the club members did was keep the neighborhood clean. Our initiation task was to pick up the trash in the alley behind the apartment buildings. My friend took one side and I took the other and we each filled a shopping bag.

The leader told us that we were not finished. He told us that we also had to pick up the dog and cat poop in the alley. That wasn't a pleasant task but when we finished, we got to walk around the neighborhood with the older boys.

We moved before I became a gang member.

Buster Bunny and the City Bus

Now, Buster Bunny was not a regular rabbit; he lived in a city. Buster had a mother Mommy, a father Daddy, an older sister Bonnie, an older brother Bobby, a younger sister Betty, and an even younger brother Baby. None of these bunnies were regular rabbits. They all lived in a city called Taleton. Most of the time, Buster was a nice kind and quiet boy bunny, but he could get into mischief with very little effort.

You may remember from other stories that Buster liked to explore. Well, most of his exploring was in the city neighborhood. One day he went a little farther than usual, but he still knew his way back. He often watched humans like Neighbor who had the garden, but he'd never seen a group of them.

They were on a hard surface we call a sidewalk. Buster watched from a shady place where a few dandelions grew between buildings. He nibbled on a few then a very large thing came near the people standing on the sidewalk. Buster was startled but saw that none of the people ran away.

One by one they got on the bus and Buster saw that the steps were not any higher than the rocks he sometimes hopped on to when playing. The last human in line stepped onto the bus and Buster made a run for it. The driver couldn't see Buster on the bottom step and closed the door.

Th motion of the bus was like nothing Buster had ever experienced. Then it stopped. Several humans were standing above him and turned toward the door next to the bottom step where he was crouched. The door opened and Buster jumped to avoid being stepped on by a large foot. He landed on the sidewalk and sprint hopped to a gap between buildings. It looked nothing like where he ate the dandelions before following the humans onto the bus.

Buster knew in an instant that he was lost, but he had no idea how to get un-lost. He hopped along the sidewalk in one direction staying as close as he could to the brick building as he could. Then he hopped the other direction and passed the narrow gap where he'd been. He continued for two city blocks and crossed streets only when humans did.

Then he saw the dandelions, one with the flower gone and the second with the flower half nibbled away. He finished the dandelion snack while thinking of what to tell Mommy why he was late getting home for supper. He knew Mommy and Daddy were clever enough to see through any story that wasn't true, so he decided truth would be the best and punishment would be the least. And he decided that if he wanted to go somewhere, he'd never been before, he should go with an older relative who knew the way home.

And, that ends another story about Buster Bunny, who was not a regular rabbit because he lived in a city.

- 8 -
Corporal Punishment

School had already started when I entered the second grade in 1943 at Moxie, WA. My migrant worker parents were picking end-of-the-season hops.

Two boys I didn't know asked me to leave the school grounds with them during lunch recess so they could buy some candy. I didn't have any money to spend but walked with them. The boys shared with me. We lost track of time and the kids were in class when we returned. When the teacher asked, we didn't lie about what we did.

He lined us up in front of the class and explained that he was going to give us a reminder. I wasn't sure what to expect. We were told to take everything out of our back pockets. Many boys had red and white plaid hankies, and a few had wallets. I had nothing so that was easy for me; but I still didn't know what to expect.

The teacher separated the first boy from us, so he was facing an open space between his desk and the students' desks. When he took a long wooden paddle from his desk drawer and said, "Reach down and touch your toes," I knew what was next.

The crack of the paddle on tightened denim was impressive as he hacked the first boy. "Did that hurt?" the teacher asked.

The boy said, "Yes sir," and was sent to his desk. It went the same for the second boy. He gave me my hack and asked the same question.

Being the new kid, being stubborn, and not wanting to appear weak. I said, "No."

The teacher hacked me several more times and after each swat he asked the same question. I gave the same answer. The pain increased with each hit and I realized that if I wanted to sit without a constant reminder I'd better say, "Yes."

I did!

He stopped!

Lessons learned!

Buster Bunny at the Park

N ow, Buster Bunny was not a regular rabbit; he lived in a city. Buster had a mother Mommy, a father Daddy, an older sister Bonnie, an older brother Bobby, a younger sister Betty, and an even younger brother Baby. None of these bunnies were regular rabbits. They all lived in a city called Taleton. Most of the time, Buster was a nice kind and quiet boy bunny, but he could get into mischief with very little effort.

[8]Buster Bunny was playing on the swing and he fell off. Brother Bobby Bunny asked him if he was OK.

Buster said, "Yes."

Mommy Bunny asked, "Is your knee bleeding?"

Buster answered, "Yes."

Mommy Bunny said, "I brought a Band-Aid for you, Buster."

Buster said, "Thank you, Mommy." He put the Band-Aid on his knee and got back on the swing, but Bobby Bunny pushed him off the swing, and Buster started to cry.

Mommy Bunny had to spank Bobby Bunny.

And, that ends another story about Buster Bunny, who was not a regular rabbit because he lived in a city.

---

[8] This story was actually made up and told by Calin.

- 9 -
Green Apples

E xpecting a long stretch of work during the summer of 1943, my parents moved from Los Angeles to a migrant camp connected to a large commercial orchard near Post Falls, Idaho. It grew several apple varieties and needed pickers for a bumper crop of an early variety. Variety planting was planned so there would be continuous picking. While the early variety was being picked, the still green apples of another variety were ripening.

Aunt Beth was an infant, so Grandma Marvel only picked a few hours a day. I was given the job of watching the younger kids at our yurt while she helped pick with the baby in a sling over her back. Many women with young kids came back to the camp to fix lunch and get a few hours out of the sun. A boy my age whose family lived in the next yurt was also tasked with watching several younger siblings.

Boys my age often replaced our mothers in the orchards – the more pickers, the more family income. The neighbor boy and I worked many mornings and some afternoons picking up culls. Pay for culls wasn't the same as for 'off the tree' but it was pay.

One hot day on the walk back to the camp for lunch that boy and I stopped at the camp well and pumped cold water on our heads. We talked about taking off our shoes and jumping into the horse watering trough next to the warehouse before we went back to picking in the afternoon. We decided to eat quickly so we could get into the cold water for a few minutes.

When I stopped at his yurt to get him, his mother told me that he died. At first, I thought it was a joke. He had hurried lunch and choked on a chunk of green apple. I've sometimes wondered about why it happened, but it was long before Heimlich and common knowledge of CPR.

I was used to never seeing someone again because they or we moved so often. That was different.

Bensons near one of the orchards in 1944.
Mother, Father, baby Beth
Lowell, Me, Connie, David

There were many camps after that. Notice the mattresses on top of the 1937 Hudson Terraplane. Uncle Arne was born in Yakama, WA, in 1945.

- 10 -
War and Blood

World War Two ended on Wednesday, August 15, 1945, and I was anticipating starting third grade in Alexandria, MN. Nearly every kid ran on Broadway that day with American flags given out by the American Legion.

My vision of the war came from comic books and movie theater newsreels on Saturday afternoons at the State Theater. Kids lined up to see cowboy or war movies where the good guys always won by doing right. Newsreels got us caught up on how the good guys were making significant advances even when outnumbered by Japanese or German soldiers.

The most convincing comic book cover I remember depicted green faced German soldiers being beaten back by a single American GI firing a machine gun with one hand and preparing to pitch a hand grenade with the other from atop a tank. Another cover showed Japanese soldiers hiding in the jungle with gull winged American fighter planes strafing and marines throwing grenades into pill boxes.

A bunch of us, tired of celebrating something we didn't fully understand, decided to play war in the open space between a gas station and our trailer house. I'm not sure if I even had shoes, if they were too small for me and hurt my feet, or if I just preferred running barefoot like many of the other boys.

I ran to attack an unseen enemy. My unseen enemy manifested as the broken base of a soda bottle. I stepped on it and it stuck in my heel. It wasn't bleeding much but it hurt enough to make me scream loudly.

A man from the gas station came outside, pulled the glass out of my foot, and blood squirted onto the driveway. I thought I was going to bleed to death. He sprayed my foot with water from the hose used for filling car radiators and wrapped it with a dipstick rag (clean I'm sure :-). Someone went to get Grandma Marvel. The man had my wound packed with another rag and ice from the soda machine by the time she got there. I don't think I went to a doctor; boy wounds were usually treated at home in those days.

We moved to Texas again, so I didn't start school in Alexandria.

I still don't like walking barefoot outside.

- 11 -
Texas Lessons

In the late summer, before school started in 1945, my father moved our faded-red trailer house from Alexandria, Minnesota, to Texas. We ended up in a trailer park on the edge of Buffalo Bayou just outside of Huston until March of the next year.

A boy my age lived in a trailer nearby. There were as many kids in his family as ours. His dad was either smoking while sitting in a chair outside their trailer or smoking and fishing from a chair on the dock extending into the bayou. It seemed to me that he also continuously sipped an amber drink from a large water glass in both places. My new friend took it upon himself to teach me lessons about a culture different from what I had known on the road.

He told me copperhead snakes from the bayou could kill a kid. That was enough warning to prevent me from teasing a sibling or someone else like I had done with garden snakes in Minnesota. I learned later, that despite the extreme discomfort from a bite, very few people die from copperhead venom.

His harshest warning was about water moccasins also called Cottonmouths. He said they could be in the water or just hanging in the tree moss ready to drop onto a passing victim. I watched the trees in the trailer park but never saw one except many years later in a movie.

He told me about alligators too. I never saw a gator but, suspecting they were lying in wait for a kid kept me well away from reeds and deep grass near the edge of the bayou.

Not all things from the bayou were bad. I learned to like catfish. Our neighbor family frequently had fried catfish with their grits for breakfast. I got my first taste when my friend shared his breakfast leftovers at school lunch. On several occasions, my friend and I were allowed to fish with his dad.

That fall I saw my first Gulf Coast water as storm surf pushed by a hurricane skirting the south Texas coast. We left the trailer park when the hurricane rain and the high seas started to push the bayou water over its banks. I'm not sure why we went to Galveston, but I was impressed by the water breaking over the sea wall and crashing onto the street that bordered the wall. When we returned days later, we saw the water marks on the bottom of the trailers and bayou debris piled under them.

I learned to call ladies ma'am and men sir at school. My trailer park friend tried to warn me, but I didn't learn the lesson until the teacher confronted me. The teacher asked me a yes or no question and I said, "Yeah." I was quickly and firmly informed that the correct response to such questions was, "Yes ma'am," or "No ma'am." Not doing so was considered inappropriate and even insulting to an adult. The tone of her message was effective! And, I also learned that y'all could be used in place of you, you all, or even all of you.

The whole class practiced for a Christmas musical. Perhaps because I was the new kid or had no apparent musical ability, my part was small and would have no impact on the program if I wasn't there. My role was to toot a small tin horn at the appropriate place in the carol "Santa Claus is Coming to Town".

> "Little tin horns, little toy drums.
> Rudy-toot-toot [toot the horn] and rummy tum tums.
> Santa Claus is coming to town."

It could have been that I didn't listen well or just couldn't hear well. I missed the cue most of the time. The teacher rebuked me in front of the class every time I missed. I don't remember being in the pageant.

The most important lesson I learned in Texas was that punishment can sometimes really fit the crime. I'm not sure if my friend learned the same lesson.

He and I walked to school together and on weekends we wandered the trailer park and nearly everywhere else except to the edge of the bayou. It was usually warm, so most people kept their doors and windows open all day long. In our wanderings we saw some kind of chocolate bar on the sill over a lady's sink.

One day we saw her leave. I don't remember whose idea it was but when she was out of sight, we ran into her trailer and grabbed two large squares of chocolate. We hid behind her trailer and ate them quickly.

Shortly later I was deservedly punished for sure! My friend probably had the same consequence.

Ex-Lax wasn't the chocolate treat we thought it was. The strong laxative did its work and the next day our mothers took us to her so we could apologize.

Buster Bunny and the Christmas Treats

N ow, Buster Bunny was not a regular rabbit; he lived in a city. Buster had a mother Mommy, a father Daddy, an older sister Bonnie, an older brother Bobby, a younger sister Betty, and an even younger brother Baby. None of these bunnies were regular rabbits. They all lived in a city called Taleton. Most of the time, Buster was a nice kind and quiet boy bunny, but he could get into mischief with very little effort.

There was a large candy factory in the city where Buster and his family lived. Every year just about Christmas time, the people at the factory would give out free candy canes and other treats to all of the children.

Well, an old rabbit that made rabbit candy heard about what the owner of the candy factory did for the children. He decided to do the same thing for the rabbits. Buster Bunny's father went to the old rabbit's store on the way home from work one day. "Do you have children at home?" the old rabbit asked Buster's father.

"Yes," he said. "In fact, my wife and I have five young bunnies at home."

"That is wonderful," the man said. "I have decided that my gift to the rabbits in the neighborhood should be to give each family some of the candy that I make in my factory."

Daddy Bunny took the candy and went home. Mommy Bunny put the candy in the cupboard until a later time when she knew it would be best to give the bunnies a treat. Well, wouldn't you just know it? Buster discovered the candy in the cupboard when he went to find dried clover for a snack. His mother told him that it was OK to have a small amount of clover or other dried flowers if he was hungry between meals.

Buster took one piece of candy.

"Boy, that was good," he said to himself. Buster found his brother Bobby Bunny and told him about the candy.

Bobby asked Buster, "Did Mother say that you could have the candy?"

"No," Buster replied, "but she didn't say we couldn't have any either." Actually, Buster had not asked if he could or could not have any of the candy.

Buster and Bobby went to the cupboard and got some more. "Boy that is good candy," Bobby said.

"I agree," said Buster. "Let's have some more."

They kept eating candy until it was almost all gone. "Maybe we should save some for the rest of the family," Bobby said.

"I don't feel so good," Buster said with a sad face.

"How much candy did you eat?" His brother asked.

Buster replied, "I don't know for sure, but I think I ate too much. My tummy really hurts."

Bobby said, "I think you should tell mother that you got sick."

Buster said, "If I do, she will know that I ate almost all of that candy."

"Just the same, Buster, I think you should. I'm going to tell her that I ate a bunch of it too. I feel bad that I did not wait and have only my share."

"I guess you are right Bobby," said Buster. "I should not have taken the first piece without asking Mommy if it was OK. I'll tell her too and perhaps when she finds out that I got sick, she will not be too angry with me."

After they told their mother, she sent Buster and Bobby to bed without any supper. She told them that she was not as upset with them as she would have been if they had not told her about taking the candy. The Bunny brothers found out that adult bunnies know best about what young bunnies should eat and about how much they should eat.

And that ends another story about Buster Bunny, who wasn't a regular rabbit because he lived in a City.

– 12 –
Kansas Twister

The spring after I was nine, we moved from Texas to a farm place in Republic County, Kansas, near the small town of Kackley.

Severe thunderstorms in Kansas are a common occurrence that time of year. The clouds rise over 40,000 feet and form what's called an anvil. Sometimes when the clouds come closer to the ground, they turn a dark greenish gray and lightning can be seen a long time before the storm arrives. Quite often, there is no rain – just lightning.

I learned to estimate the distance to the lightning strike by counting seconds between the flash and the sound of thunder. Sound travels about one mile a second so one-second between flash and sound is one mile. Of course, that only works if there is just one lightning bolt. When they came close in sequence, and they very often did in Kansas, it was hard to tell which one I saw first.

Sheet lightning reminded me of clouds being spotted with anti-aircraft beacons in Los Angeles during the war. The cloud to cloud lightning strikes sometimes happened so often that they gave enough continuous light for us to find our way to the outhouse. Sometimes I wondered what would happen if the outhouse got hit by a lightning bolt when I was inside.

Many times, during a thunderstorm the wind would swirl and change from hot to cold blasts. When clouds were low and blackish green, local radio stations issued tornado watches or warnings and the birds got silent. I wondered what we would do if one of the tornados we saw in the distance came our way. We didn't have a storm shelter on that farm.

Then I wondered no more. A tornado passed very, very close to our house in the dark. I still remember the roar. Some people have described the sound as like being within a few feet of a speeding train. I had not been that close to a fast-moving train, but now the description sounds like what I remember.

It was hot and humid so the windows in the house were open. The vacuum caused by the twister pulled curtains from the windows and the top sheets from the bed where we boys were sleeping. We didn't find them until morning. They were tangled in the twisted and broken trees in the windbreak about 50 feet from the house. The house wasn't damaged but the wheat field on the other side of the windbreak was flattened.

I found out later that having the windows open during a tornado is a good thing. The difference in atmospheric pressure inside and outside can cause windows to break and walls explode.

Uncle Ronald was born in Kansas on July 7, 1946.

- 12 -
Van Hook

Van Hook is now a ghost town in Van Hook Township, Mountrail County, North Dakota. The original town site was flooded when the Garrison Dam was built, and Lake Sakakawea was formed in the 1950s.

We lived with Grandma Josine Benson at the Van Hook Bell Telephone Office a few weeks until Grandma Marvel rented the Wilber[9] house at the west edge of town. We lived there from the fall of 1946 to the end of school in 1949. Summers were very hot, dusty and windy. Winters were very cold, snowy and windy.

We had a cave but not like the one in the Tom Sawyer story. Ours was an abandoned lignite mine under the 'cliff' where snow cornices formed in the winter. It only went in about thirty or forty feet, so except for a few feet from where it ended, we could always see the entrance from inside. The cliff was about 20 feet high but seemed much higher to us. In our minds, the mine begged to be explored; and, we did.

---

[9] The water behind Garrison Dam rose and the Corps of Engineers bought the Wilber's house for $4,000 and they purchased it back for about $1,500. They paid $300 to have it moved into New Town, ND, in 1953.

It wasn't permitted but sometimes we would walk the mile out of town to the rodeo grounds and throw cow chips. There was an alkali pond near the rodeo grounds that was also on the forbidden list. A few times we snuck in a swim (dog paddle).

The railroad tracks provided entertainment too. We used the weight of trains to flatten pennies on the rails. Someone told us that if a train hit a bump as small as a coin it could be derailed. We didn't believe that, but we could get two pieces of Double-Bubble for a penny, so it wasn't too often that we had one flattened. I wonder sometimes how many rare coins became wafer thin copper. Another railroad thing was to accept a challenge to walk a rail farther than someone else. There had to be a witness of course to verify bragging rights.

For the most part, winter was more fun for kids because we didn't understand the consequence of poor decisions in that hostile environment. The school being closed for storms was far more fun for us than for the adults.

The town made a skating rink each winter and many of us spent weekend daylight hours there. Boys spent some winter evenings and Saturdays at the boxing club.

Sledding was a universal activity in the winter because no snow was rarer than no wind. The surface of the snow was often so wind-whipped that its crust was thick with very few soft spots and perfect for sledding. We could even jump off our outhouse roof and not break through to the crystal-like snow under the crust. The snow frequently drifted high enough so all we had to do is stand on the steering bar of a sled to get on top.

- 13 -
Girls of Van Hook

G irls are not a big part of my memories of Van Hook. Laura Lea Prior, Mary Ellen Traynor and the one who was often asked to sing at events. I don't remember her name but the song she sang at school and other places was always "Beautiful Dreamer."

Looking Southwest into Van Hook from the Wilber house. Laura Lea Prior is holding Ronald. Lowell and Arne are in the background

It seems that every time Mrs. Prior visited Grandma Marvel, her daughter Laura Lea was along. I think she was a little older than me, but perhaps not. For some reason, I've always thought she was a cousin, but I was wrong about the Ranum boys too.

Sometimes we had an older girl babysitter. The only one whose name I remember is the neighbor Denelda Lundstedt. When we had others, I probably just went somewhere to read if we were being watched, so I have no recall of who they might have been.

– 14 –
Running Water

Plumbing as we know it was rare in rural North Dakota in the late 1940s. The Wilber house Grandma Marvel rented was one of the newest in town, but it wasn't plumbed either. I'm not sure if anyone in Van Hook had running water in their homes. One small room in the house was the bathroom in name only. It didn't have a sink, tub, shower or toilet. Grandma Marvel used the little room for storage and hanging washed clothing for drying in the winter.

We washed up in the kitchen, took a bath in a galvanized washtub, rinsed off in a second tub and the outhouse was the toilet. The kitchen sink drained into a five-gallon pail. We used kitchen drain water and the used bath water on the garden and for the two little trees Grandma Marvel had planted on the side of the house. They didn't survive her TLC.

Grandma Marvel heated water from the cistern for the ringer washing machine and drained it with a hose to the garden plot in the spring and summer. In the winter it was drained wherever the hose reached outside.

I didn't think about how the town might have supplied the stores and taverns with water, but the railroad station and the school had an indoor flush toilet and a drinking fountain. I was never inside either of the taverns or the restaurant so I wouldn't have known about them. Some families had their own well and some like our neighbors the Olson brothers[10] even had an electric pump.

Uncle Lowell and I pulled our rusted Radio Flyer wagon a half mile to the city pump by the railroad station to fill one of our two ten-gallon milk cans with drinking and cooking water in the spring, summer and fall. Some of the other town kids had that chore too but most people went to the well with their car or pickup truck.

The pump spout was high enough and long enough so we could pull the wagon with the can underneath it and fill it directly from the pump. There was a little set of stairs and a very small platform so short people and kids could reach the handle. A summer trip to the well was usually fun because we could pump cold water on our heads and sometimes, we splashed cold water from the can onto ourselves while we pulled the wagon home.

Someone in the town put up a portable shed to shelter the pump before freezing temperatures set in. They put an electric heater around the pump and pipe so it wouldn't freeze. There was nothing that would keep the spilled water

---

[10] John Geoffrey and Hubert L. (Goff and Hub) Olson were bachelor brothers who shared their farm home. Hub was the Van Hook postmaster and Goff operated the farm. Both were very kind to us. When we first met them in 1946, Goff was 57 and Hub was 55.

from freezing and the little pump house floor always had ice on it. We knew enough to wear gloves when touching the pump handle, but even damp gloves would stick to the surface. An earlier tongue on clothesline-post frost experience was enough for me. (Many of you will remember the triple dog dare incident in the movie *A Christmas Story.*)

Now and then someone would chip the ice away and put some salted sand on the surface, so it wasn't so slippery. Several snowfalls left the floor inside the pump house lower than the packed snow on the street. We couldn't pull the sled inside the pump house anyway and Uncle Lowell and I together couldn't lift ten gallons of water. We had to use a bucket to fill it. Our frequent spills contributed to the ice below the pump. Water spilled inside a shoe or overshoe was no fun either.

One time it was so cold that even though the water sloshed around in the can we pulled on the Flexible Flyer, ice formed on the top of the water by the time we got it home. Another time, we got almost home, and the sled hit some grit on the road and stopped suddenly. Neither of us was holding on to the can so it tipped over. The water spilled and we had to go back to the pump.

We didn't use water from the town pump for bathing or even washing dishes. We and nearly everyone else had a cistern. Some people's cisterns were a sealed concrete tank under their house. Ours was an open top tank like farmers use to water their livestock. It sat on a dirt platform in the cellar. A sheet metal lined ditch ran under the house to route summer rain or spring snow melt into it. I'm not sure what kept the cistern from running over – I never saw water on the cellar floor. It had a slatted wall between its top and the floor joists and a door that Grandma Marvel kept locked. She must have suspected that one of us might have thought about taking a dip in it.

Three sides of the cellar were dirt and the wall around the cistern served as the fourth wall where Grandma Marvel stored her home canned fruit on shelves under the stairs. She kept her home canned vegetables on shelves nailed to the side of the coal bin.

Corn in the jars was the color of a manila folder and the green beans should have been called gray beans. The peas didn't keep their natural color any better than the beans. Canned beets were my favorite winter vegetable, but most of the family didn't like them. I often put them under my mashed potatoes to see how long it took to turn the potatoes red. I didn't care that much for the juice, but it made the coloring go faster. The fruit looked a little better. I liked the whole crab apples because the skin was crunchy.

A small hand pump next to the kitchen sink had to be primed and then we could pump up enough water for washing. Cistern water wasn't used for cooking or drinking but I used to catch a cup full now and then when I was priming the pump. Grandma Marvel told me that someone in town found a snake in their cistern, so remembering one of my Texas lessons, I stopped sipping from ours. The cistern was usually dry before the spring thaw, so we brought snow inside and melted it in a tub next to the furnace for washing and our weekly bath.

We moved to Minnesota before public running water and a public sewer system was available to homes in Van Hook. Then, as I said earlier, the town was forced away by the Garrison Dam.

- 15 -
Michael Fitzpatrick

Michael Fitzpatrick was the first kid I met in Van Hook and may have been the last one I saw before we left. Right away he told me he didn't like being called Fitz. I didn't but many of the boys and even some adults called him Fitz. Michael was as skinny as me but a little taller and he could whistle a tune with his pointer and little fingers. He was in my classroom for three grades at the only school in Van Hook. We were in the boxing club and explored the lignite cave together.

Most boys wore blue denim bibs; mine were mail order or hand-me-downs from generous parents of older kids in town. Michael always wore striped Oshkosh bib overalls for school and play. Oshkosh was the premium brand. No one wore overalls or jeans to church – we had to wear slacks or corduroy pants.

Michael and his family went to St. Anthony Catholic Church, so I never saw him in dress clothing because we went to Bethany Lutheran Church. Changing out of church outfits was demanded on Sunday before lunch so they'd be in good condition more than one week in a row. The only exception to that rule was if there was an after-church potluck or picnic.

I wasn't sure Michael's father existed until I learned that he owned the tavern where we turned in collected beer bottles. Michael's mother was thin like Michael and always wore flour sack dresses like the women in the movie *The Grapes of Wrath*. Mrs. Fitzpatrick's most used expression was, "Michael, if you don't listen to me (do what I tell you) (don't do that) (stop cursing) (etc.) I'm going to send you to Boys' Town."

Michael was always looking for some kind of adventure and trying to convince someone to share mischief with him. Michael was the kid who had firecrackers before the others. He even had cherry bombs we used to launch number ten cans into the air. When he would tell me that he had better get home, or had better do his chores, or something else he nearly always ended with, "or sheee's gonna send me to Boys' Town."

I always wondered if she was going to send him on a train or take him there herself. We all knew about Father Flanagan's Boys' Town because of the movie with Mickey Rooney. I don't think I ever saw it, but I read the signs outside the theater.

The theater in Van Hook had movies only on Friday night, Saturday afternoon and Saturday night. A kid could see the Saturday matinée for a dime and a nickel would buy a large bag of popcorn.

There was talk among the men at the boxing club matches about one movie that our mothers wouldn't let us go see. It was *The Outlaw* with Jane Russell.

Knowing that it was on the prohibited list, Michael plotted a way to sneak into the theater. We pooled our money and gave it to Keith Ranum because he was older. The plan was for him to buy his ticket with our money and open the back door to let us in. Keith either got caught or changed his mind once he got inside. We waited by the back-exit listening until long after the news and selected short subjects were shown. We gave up. He never did tell us about the movie and why we should not have seen it.

Ron Grendahl and Stan Rust were in school with Michael and me. Stan lived on a farm, so he wasn't a playmate during the summer. Michael plotted tricks on teachers, but Ron and I didn't go along with him. I don't remember if Stan went along or not. Not having an accomplice didn't seem to bother Michael; he did mischief on his own.

Ron was also in my Sunday school class. He was probably the best fed kid I knew but he wasn't fat. Ron supplied the bat and baseball and sometimes gloves when we went to the school grounds to play ball. He was catching when I got beaned by Dale Babcock.

Ron's dad was the local barber but I'm not sure if he or a relative owned Grendahl's Grocery where Grandma Marvel had a 'tab'.

Grandma Marvel drove our 1939 Mercury into the front window of the store. I didn't know it had happened until Ron told Michael and Michael ran to our house and told me. We ran across town to see. The car had been pulled back onto the street so all we saw was the gaping hole where the big window and door had been.

I last saw Michael Fitzpatrick at the back of his father's tavern the day before we left Van Hook in 1949 when I turned in bottles I had collected. I've always wondered what happened to Michael. [11]

---

[11] Keith read this and several other of my stories on my blog and contacted me. He said he didn't remember many of the things that happened some 70 years before. He mentioned that he had ran into Michael Fitzpatrick at a New Town reunion. New Town was formed by people from Van Hook and Sanish when waters from the Garrison Dam covered the towns in the early 1950s.

– 16 –
Chicken Bones

O ur neighbor Mr. Lundstedt frequently used an old axe grinder behind his tool shed to grind his axe razor sharp. The grinder had a large stone wheel in a frame with a seat. It was operated by a system similar to a

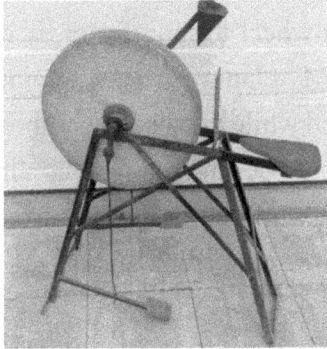

Not the one, but it looked like this.

child peddle car and the axe or hatchet was moved perpendicular to the spinning wheel.

The sharpening wheel was kept cool by dripping water from a small can fastened to the frame. I tried several times, but Mr. Lundstedt finished for me each time I tried to sharpen our hatchet. I couldn't hold the hatchet firmly enough to get a consistent edge and he didn't condone a dull edge.

One hot day when he wasn't home, I decided to see how fast I could get the wheel spinning in reverse so the water from the drip can would spray on my face. I moved it as fast as I could with the pedals, but the water only sprayed on my chest. I disconnected the rods that connected the pedals to the cranks on either side of the wheel. I turned the crank on one side by hand. I made it go faster and faster when it was unrestricted by the pedal mechanism.

I had a plan. I tried spinning it with one pedal attached. I could still get the wheel turning faster by cranking than by using the pedals. My plan was to get it going really fast then attach the pedal rod while the wheel was moving. At the right speed my face would be sprayed with cooling water.

My plan didn't work the first time I tried. My right little finger caught between the crank and axle.

Rip!

Pain!

The wheel stopped and I unwound my finger from the mechanism. The skin on the palm side held my finger on and the knuckle of the separated joint was exposed. It looked just like the bone ends from a chicken leg. I put the rod back on with my left hand.

I pushed the bones together, so they looked right and closed the skin over the top. There was very little bleeding. I ran home. I put a small piece of cloth from Grandma Marvel's sewing kit over the skin flap and taped it as tight as I could. Mother didn't pay much attention to it. With seven kids wounding themselves on a regular basis there wasn't need for concern, except when an injury was brought to her attention.

Knowing I would be in trouble for using the axe grinder without Mr. Lundstedt's being present, I kept it well hidden and didn't complain. I'm not sure if it was the second or third day when Grandma Marvel noticed that my hand was swollen. Somehow, she got me to Parshall, ten miles from Van Hook, to see the doctor (the son of the Dr. Blatherwick who had delivered me in Sanish).

He looked at it, put a small splint on my finger and said he couldn't do much else at that point. I took off the splint and soaked it in warm water several times a day until the swelling went down.

Sometimes when my hand gets really cold, I feel a little ache in that joint, but other than that it has never bothered me, except when I see an axe grinder and the memory is rekindled.

Buster Bunny at His Father's Work

Now, Buster Bunny was not a regular rabbit; he lived in a city. Buster had a mother Mommy, a father Daddy, an older sister Bonnie, an older brother Bobby, a younger sister Betty, and an even younger brother Baby. None of these bunnies were regular rabbits. They all lived in a city called Taleton. Most of the time, Buster was a nice kind and quiet boy bunny, but he could get into mischief with very little effort.

It was "bring your child to work day" at Daddy's work. Mommy Bunny told Daddy that Buster had been good for the last week and that it was OK for him to go.

Bobby and Bonnie were in bunny school and had gone to work with Daddy when they were the same age as Buster. Betty and Baby were too young to go to their father's work and Mr. and Mrs. Bunny had been given permission from the school for Buster to be absent that day.

Buster was double excited the morning he was going to work with Daddy. Both Bobby and Bonnie had told him how much fun they had when it was their turn and he did not have to go to school. It was not that he did not like school but he knew that Teacher was going to show a movie because so many bunnies would not be there, and he had already seen the movie several times.

He and his friends had talked about what they would get to do at work and some of the others asked if they could go to work with Buster's father because their fathers worked in offices. Buster's father worked in a little shop where they repaired spectacles.

Buster was amazed at all of the little parts in the little bins and how his father knew the name of each and on what kind of glasses they fit. Each of the other workers had his or her supply of parts. Buster watched his father and the others replacing parts and straightening bent parts on all kinds of glasses. It was nearly quitting time and one of the workers went on break and Buster thought that he had learned enough by watching to fix a pair of glasses himself. He had totally forgotten that he had been told to not touch any tools or parts.

Well, if you know Buster you will know that this is where the trouble starts. He took the next pair in the row of glasses to be fixed and examined it as if he knew what he was doing. The first pair just needed a screw tightened and Buster did that, smiled with pride in himself and then took the next pair from the row. There was a screw missing and Buster selected one he thought would fit.

He started the screw and when it seemed to be hard to turn with the little screwdriver, he applied more force. The screw still did not turn, and he tried harder. The screwdriver blade slipped, and Buster poked his hand causing it to bleed. When he cried, his father noticed what he had been doing.

Fortunately for Buster, his father was able to fix the problem that Buster had caused and with a small bandage on his finger he apologized to the other worker and learned that he should listen to his father's instructions.

And that ends another story about Buster Bunny, who wasn't a regular rabbit because he lived in the City.

- 17 -
Shot in the Arm

G randma Marvel said that she wanted to have a small garden in the open space between our place and the Olson farm just up the hill. Mr. Olson plowed the packed soil and prairie grass for her. She used a spade to turn over the furrows and asked me to break up the clumps with a hoe and rake it smooth so she could plant.

I was chopping hard and suddenly my left arm went limp; it just hung at my side. It was really a strange feeling. I thought I had twisted it by hitting the sod too hard with the hoe. I lifted my skinny arm and turned it with my right hand to see what was wrong.

A small trickle of blood ran down my arm. I examined it and saw a gray object sticking out about halfway between my shoulder and elbow. I released my limp arm and it fell like a loose rope. There was still no feeling. By the time I got the hundred feet or so to the house, it started to tingle like an arm recovering from having been slept on all night.

I looked for my mother, but she wasn't home. I pulled out the object myself with a pair of tweezers. There was only a little more bleeding. I swabbed the wound with rubbing alcohol and felt the burning sting.

The object was a twenty-two-caliber bullet, but I had not heard a shot. I saved the bullet to show Grandma Marvel when I told her what had happened. I could move all of my fingers so that was the end of it.

I learned later that a .22 long rifle round could travel nearly a mile.

- 18 -
Shot to the Head

I didn't get shot in the head – I took a shot to the head. Baseball was the sport boys and men in Van Hook played most. There were no organized teams for boys our age so we played wherever we could find a game, but I don't remember any girls playing sports.

The spring of my fifth-grade year I was old enough to play with the older kids as a fill in. I was filled with pride when I got to bat against Dale Babcock. Dale was only in the ninth grade but to us he looked like a giant and had a sports hero reputation. He pitched for one of the adult town league teams. I didn't have much trouble hitting the ball against kids my own age but no one our age expected to ever hit a pitch delivered by him.

I could feel the wind as the ball went by the first time. I moved the bat off my shoulder as Dale's arm moved towards the catcher, but the ball was already in Ron Grendahl's mitt by the time I had the bat in the air. An older boy told me to keep the bat off my shoulder and lean a little forward so I wouldn't have to move the bat so far to hit.

Dale's arm was at the top of his pitching arc, so I leaned forward as instructed. The path of the ball was exactly where he intended, but he didn't know that I would move my head into its path.

I was hit so hard that my feet went into the air and I fell on my back. I remember having a knot on my head for the rest of the day. It was a lot worse than the haymaker I got from a boxing club opponent but not as bad as the impact from my falling on the ice.

No one blamed Dale for beaning me - and neither did I. After all, I leaned into the pitch and he put it right where he intended.

I gave up baseball and even softball for a long time. I just couldn't bring myself to stand up at the plate even in casual slow pitch games as an adult.

- 19 -
Flying Upside Down

My father took me flying in a small two-seater, single wing, Piper Cub several years before we were in Van Hook. He sat in front and I sat behind him. The overhead wing and large clear plastic side curtains made it easy for me to see outside of the airplane. But I wondered how a pilot could drive because when the 'tail dragger' was on the ground all he could see through the windshield was the sky. When my father started to move on the runway, he leaned out the side curtain and I wondered if he had to do that in the air too.

I don't know if my father had a pilot license, but he knew how to fly an airplane. I learned later that he had learned to fly a glider when he was in high school. He and some of his high school friends built a working, one seat glider and allegedly flew it off Mt. Crow Flies High near Sanish, ND. I also heard a story about them pulling it with a car and rope to get it off the ground.

There was a man in Van Hook who took people for rides in his tandem open cockpit Waco biplane. I was probably eleven the first time he took me up; I sat in the front seat. I couldn't figure why or how he could drive from the back seat. I didn't realize until much later that it was for balance and that flying was much different from driving a car. He told me that he could actually see the ground better from the rear cockpit because the forward one was over the lower wing.

He also explained that the Waco had dual controls in each cockpit and cautioned me to not touch any of them. He told me that I could tell if we were climbing, descending, or if the wings were out of parallel to the ground by looking at the tiny silhouette in the bubble on the control panel.

The second time I went up in the biplane, the man did several stunts, which I enjoyed at least as much as going on rides at the carnival that stopped in Van Hook that summer. The snap rolls rattled my head but after a few I got used to it. The regular loop-the-loops put a pressure on my stomach that I had not experienced before. The most exciting thing to me was when he did an outside loop over the town dump.

The best I can describe it is to compare it to being on a 2,000-foot high Ferris wheel and having the seat locked at the top of the circle (going much, much faster of course). When the wheel turns toward the ground the seat doesn't turn and by the time you are at the bottom, all that is holding you in is your seat belt. Of course, we had shoulder straps also, but it still felt very strange tipping my head to what was normally up to look down. The feeling in my stomach was the opposite of the inside loop feeling. I wondered where the result of my upchucking would land if I actually did. Maybe that's why he did the outside loop over the town dump.

I still remember the change in the sound of the powerful radial engine when he took the plane straight up until it stalled and came over backwards. At that time, I really wanted to become a pilot but the closest I ever got was building and flying models.

The last time I went up with him was about the same as the second time. He did some stunts and it was just as much fun, but I had more confidence, so I wasn't as afraid. However, when we landed on the airstrip that was more like a field, one of his wheels caught in a rut and we nosed over and broke the propeller.

That was as sudden a stop as I have ever had until I crashed my neighbor's pickup when I was a teenager.

John F Benson w / friends and glider

- 20 -
Pocket Change

I t was rare for most kids in Van Hook to have more than a few cents in their pockets. We were the seven 'on relief' kids at the edge of town so it was even rarer for us. Uncle Lowell, Uncle David and I found ways to get some money and Grandma Marvel allowed us to keep what we got.

We would walk the ditches from our side of town to the other looking for beer or soda bottles. Regular size bottles were worth one or two cents and quart beer bottles were worth a nickel.

Beer bottles were turned in at the back door of Fitzpatrick's Tavern and we got change for the soda bottles at Grendahl's Grocery. Sometimes we turned the soda bottles in at the Farmer's Union gas station. Many times, our walk would get us about twenty cents to divide between the three of us. Our best bottle collecting days were after most of the snow melted and exposed bottles that had been hidden for months.

We often pulled our well used Radio Flyer wagon with us so if we found some scrap metal, we could turn it in at the Farmer's Union. The man who ran the station collected scrap metal in the back of a truck until he had a load to take somewhere – probably Minot. He paid a half a cent per pound for steel and iron and more for brass and copper. One time we found a car battery and he gave us a dollar for it.

One August our neighbor Goff Olson gave us jobs helping him harvest his grain. I'm sure to this day that he didn't need the help but gave each of us a two-week long job. He paid me two dollars a day to drive the tractor pulling the combine. Uncle Lowell got one dollar a day to keep the grain spout clean and Uncle David got fifty cents a day to stay away from the machines.

Uncle Lowell and I both sold copies of *Grit Magazine* and tins of Cloverline Salve our second summer in Van Hook. *Grit Magazine* was a national news magazine but was sold mostly in rural America. We got the *Grit* in the mail twice a month and sold it door to door. Sometimes our profit was just the left-over copies of the paper because other kids in town were also selling the news journal. Cloverline Salve sales were just about as non-profitable. It was a good product, but it lasted a long time and in a town of 300, the market was soon saturated by multiple kids selling it. Grandma Marvel still had several cans of Cloverline when we moved to Minnesota the next year.

One of my favorite things to do with pocket change was to exchange it for a dollar bill.

- 21 -
Captain Confident

My ten-year-old imagination was triggered by comic books showing Superman and Captain Marvel leaping into the air. In the Saturday matinée movies at Van Hook's theater, I saw them take a run to get started.

An abandoned church basement in the space between our outhouse and the Lundstedt place was off limits for playing. It filled with snow and after it melted, Mr. Lundstedt removed the temptation for boys to take a swim when he pumped the water into a tank for his garden.

Whomever abandoned it left the floor joists and a wood floor over most of the basement. The exposed joists were close enough for us boys to swing from one to the next when playing Tarzan. If we missed, it was a long drop to the concrete floor but no farther than flying off a swing at the school grounds.

One day I decided that I could run across the partly finished floor, grab a joist, and swing through a rectangular opening in the basement wall which was probably there for a door or window.

I knew I had to jump over one or two joists, go between the next to the last and grab onto the last one before swinging through the opening. I practiced by running near the edge of the floor and turning just before making the jump. I felt confident that I could do the maneuver.

I used one of Grandma Marvel's flower sack dish towels for a cape and took a hard run to get started. Wham!

Hitting the wall just below the opening, I slid down the unfinished concrete scraping my chest raw.

Acting on one's imagination can be dangerous.

Buster Bunny and the Parking Lot

Now, Buster Bunny was not a regular rabbit; he lived in a city. Buster had a mother Mommy, a father Daddy, an older sister Bonnie, an older brother Bobby, a younger sister Betty, and an even younger brother Baby. None of these bunnies were regular rabbits. They all lived in a city called Taleton. Most of the time, Buster was a nice kind and quiet boy bunny, but he could get into mischief with very little effort.

The human person supermarket was just a short distance from where Buster's family lived. Mommy and sometimes Daddy took the children along to find cabbages and other greens that some human decided would not sell. Most of the time the throw-away vegetables were in a very large blue thing that no rabbit could get into. Humans call them Dumpsters, but there is no word for them in rabbit language.

Sometimes when the large blue things were nearly full, boxes or bags of eatables were stacked alongside of them. Those days were glorious for all the rabbit families in the neighborhood. Every bunny got plenty to eat and no human cared if each rabbit carried some to their burrow.

Buster was full and bored, so he decided to watch the human children leaving the store with their parents. Those who seemed to be older walked ahead or behind their parents. Those who were smaller were held onto by an older human child or a parent. Buster wondered why they couldn't just go without being held onto like he Bobby, Bonnie, Betty, and even Baby were allowed to walk on their own. Well, he was about to find out.

It goes without saying that the majority of bunnies never go to the store and therefore don't even know about parking lots. After watching the human children for a while, Buster saw something at the base of a small tree at the end of a row of things the parents and children were getting into. He took a long hop and went into sprint mode to get to what he thought might be clover under the little tree.

Rabbits have very good, actually excellent hearing which is better than very good. The screech was loud enough to make Buster do a hop higher than he ever had before. He looked up and there was a monster one of those things the humans were getting in and out of hovering over him. He quivered as it moved slowly away in the opposite direction it had been moving.

Buster turned and sprint hopped to his mother. She explained that parking lots could be dangerous even for human children.

And, that ends another story about Buster Bunny, who was not a regular rabbit because he lived in a city.

- 22 -
Summer Wind

O uthouses being tipped over was the sort of thing that happened on Halloween nights when teenage boys roamed Van Hook with nothing else to do. Outhouses being tipped over was the sort of thing that happened when tornadoes ripped through or very near Van Hook several times when we lived there.

One night a tornado came close to our house. The roar woke me up just like the one in Kansas. It tipped over our outhouse and moved it a good distance from the pit. It's a good thing no one went out there until daylight. A neighbor's house wasn't damaged either, but their outhouse was also tipped over.

The storm blew away the haystack next to Goff Olson's barn to the north of us, but it didn't damage any of his buildings. Even his outhouse was left standing. A dozen round, corrugated steel, temporary storage units by the railroad tracks, about a quarter mile down the hill to the south from us, sustained the most visible damage. The tornado crumpled them like aluminum soda cans stomped on by a playing boy. Boys my age spent hours playing in and around them and being amazed at how all of the wheat was gone.

Another tornado that summer hit the south side of town and lifted a wooden grain storage building from its foundation but there was no other damage. The tornado turned the building almost precisely 180 degrees and set it back on its foundation. Adults talked about how little or none of the grain was lost.

We boys were quite impressed when we saw the entry door with no steps and the steps and loading ramps on the other side with no doors.

Buster Bunny and the Lumber Yard

Now, Buster Bunny was not a regular rabbit; he lived in a city. Buster had a mother Mommy, a father Daddy, an older sister Bonnie, an older brother Bobby, a younger sister Betty, and an even younger brother Baby. None of these bunnies were regular rabbits. They all lived in a city called Taleton. Most of the time, Buster was a nice kind and quiet boy bunny, but he could get into mischief with very little effort.

Bobby and Bonnie were in school so they couldn't visit their grandparents except weekends and during the summer. Betty and Baby were too young to visit without Mommy being there too. But Buster was just the right age to spend a weekday with Grandpa Billings and Grandma Brianna.

Buster's grandparents lived next to a lumber yard in a rabbit village some distance from Taleton. The lumber yard wasn't a people lumber yard, but it did the same thing for bunnies. Daddy's brother Uncle Bob for whom Bobby was named worked there.

As you might suspect, Buster was curious about what went on at the yard. When Uncle went back to work after lunch, Buster followed him at a distance he was sure Uncle wouldn't see him. And he didn't.

People lumber yards have nearly everything dads need for projects and what builders need for building. Bunny lumber yards have what bunnies need for building or disguising their shelters. Bunnies who don't have soft ground to dig a burrow must gather shelter materials but getting them at a bunny lumber yard may save them time and effort.

Buster didn't know about stores or other places that sell things. Where he lived in the city, he watched Mommy gather things to make their home cozy and safe. Well, you guessed it! Buster, thinking he could help Grandma make her home better, decided to gather as many things as he could. Buster went from stacks of sticks and stacks of straw and stacks of other materials he'd seen at home. Then he found the fluff bin. The smell reminded him of where he slept in their city burrow. You guessed it! What reminded him of sleep made him sleepy.

After a very long nap, Buster gathered what he could carry of his collection and headed for Grandma and Grandpa's burrow. He put everything in front of the opening and rushed inside to tell of his gift.

Grandma was surprised, but not pleased. "Buster," she said. "Where did you get these things?"

Buster had heard the same tone of voice from his mother. He hesitated then explained, "everything was just stacked neatly where Uncle works, and I thought you could use what I brought for you."

Grandma asked, "Buster, does your father get paid for working?"

"Yes Grandma," he answered.

"Well Uncle Bob gets paid too. His pay comes from what is sold at the lumber yard. So, if someone takes things without paying, his boss might not have enough to pay him. Everything needs to go back, and I will help you. You must also tell Uncle's boss you didn't know and are sorry for what you did.

Uncle and his boss accepted Buster's apology and Buster never took too keep anything that wasn't his again.

And, that ends another story about Buster Bunny, who was not a regular rabbit because he lived in a city.

- 23 -
Summer Fire

D dry lightning storm started a prairie fire just about a quarter mile west of our rented place. The town siren alerted the volunteer fire department – nearly every man in town. Many times, before the prairie fire the siren had been a signal for curious kids to run to watch the volunteers save a building.

We arrived one or two at a time depending how far we had to run. The day of the prairie fire the Ranum boys and I arrived first. Some women were already using wet gunny sacks to smack the burning grass, so we grabbed sacks and followed their lead.

An east wind blew the smoke and fire away from town when it started but the wind changed direction and the fire started moving our way. Van Hook's only fire truck moved along the spreading fire line and men sprayed water, but they couldn't keep up with the wind fanned fire. The fire line just got longer so by the time the truck got to one end, the matted grass was aflame at the other end. Someone pulled a water tank truck near the fire line so the fire truck could refill its tank.

During refill time the fire gained ground towards town. Another person pulled a small water trailer to the fire site.

When our sacks got nearly dry, we ran to the smaller water trailer to get the sack wet again and put our head under the spout to cool off. As soon as the fire truck tank was filled someone drove the water tanker back to the town well to be filled again. But it was slow filling from the manual town pump, then someone thought about the water tower used to replace water in steam engines near the railroad station.

It looked to me like the fire was making more progress than we were. Goff Olson appeared on the scene with his old cog wheel John Deer tractor pulling a twelve-foot wide eight-bottom plow. He drove the tractor and plow parallel to the fire line between us and the edge of town. Goff and his powerful tractor kept the plow moving at a slow but steady pace through the unbroken sod.

He made two or three runs before the fire could advance to where he started. We kept the fire down until he turned over enough sod to break up the fuel source. His action may have saved the town or at least our home.

Burning prairie grass has a strange smell. The smell is not the same as clinkers[12] and ashes on snow, but once you experience it, the smell is hard to forget. The next day it rained without lightning and wind.

---

[12] noun. the ash and partially fused residues from a coal-fired furnace or fire.

- 24 -
Cowboys and Indians

Influenced by the western movies and comic books of the 1940s we often played cowboys and Indians with our friends in Van Hook. And, except for Tonto and Little Beaver, the Indians were always the bad guys.

We had cap pistols, Daisy BB guns, rubber knives, and homemade bows. We always made sure the BB guns were out of BBs before we used them against each other. Most of us had shot at least one bird and knew they were dangerous if used against a person. Indian players only shot imaginary arrows with their bows for the same reason.

Our cousins, Dale, Neil and Robert Olson[13] were visiting so we and some other boys chose sides and set up for a fun afternoon of fake battle. Uncle Lowell was one of the Indians. We had been playing for several hours and we cowboys were out of caps. We barricaded ourselves behind our Radio Flyer wagon and some cardboard boxes and they had us surrounded.

Uncle Lowell ran to change his position in the ditch alongside the road holding the Daisy above his head like a charging Brave we had seen in the movies.

---

[13] My cousins were not related to Goff and Hub Olson.

I threw my cap pistol at him as he ran. I didn't lead him so I knew it would land behind him. Just as it left my hand, he stopped and aimed the Daisy at us. My timing would have been great if he had not stopped running.

My cap pistol hit him smack on the forehead just as he dry-fired the BB gun. His war-whoop changed to a yell of pain and surprise. He dropped his gun and held his head. It was the first real wound of the game and we all ran to see if he was OK.

He survived. Grandma Marvel gave him a cold rag for the bump on his head and sentenced me to weed the garden while the other boys played.

The cowboys, out of ammo and outnumbered, lost the game.

The day we played cowboys and Indians someone took this picture. Cousin Dale is aiming the BB gun with the BB tube removed. Aunt Connie in front of Great-Aunt Elizabeth is hidden behind Uncle Lowell. Grandma Marvel wasn't restraining me – just resting her arm. Aunt Beth, Cousin Neil, Uncle David and Cousin Robert are in the front. Goff and Hub Olson's farm is in the background.

Buster Bunny and His Sister's Toys

N ow, Buster Bunny was not a regular rabbit; he lived in a city. Buster had a mother Mommy, a father Daddy, an older sister Bonnie, an older brother Bobby, a younger sister Betty, and an even younger brother Baby. None of these bunnies were regular rabbits. They all lived in a city called Taleton. Most of the time, Buster was a nice kind and quiet boy bunny, but he could get into mischief with very little effort.

One day Buster was having a mean streak. This was not at all like Buster. All of his brothers and sisters, except Baby, of course, were outside playing. Buster did not want to be outside, but he did not want to be inside either. To be sure, he did not know what he wanted to be doing or where he wanted to be.

Where the idea to hide Sister Bonnie's toys came from, he did not know. However, that is just what he decided to do.

First, he took all of her dolls and the doll dresses and the doll hats and the doll shoes and loaded them into her doll buggy. He wheeled them into his room and hid everything except the buggy under Brother Bobby's bed.

Then Buster went back to the girls' room and found most of Bonnie's other toys and hid them under Baby's crib. Then he put the doll buggy behind the kitchen door that was always open in the summertime.

Mommy called everyone in to clean up for supper. Because he was already inside, Buster was first bunny to the table. Mother put Baby in his highchair and Daddy sat in the large chair at the head of the table. Mommy waited until everyone was around the table before she served the dinner of fresh clover and other wild greens.

After dinner Daddy said, "OK, little bunnies, you may play inside or read your books for a while before you go to bed."

Because Baby was a messy eater, bathing him after supper was a routine activity. Mommy and Daddy put baby bunny in his crib in their room. The boy bunnies went to their room and the girl bunnies went to their room.

Betty found some of her toys and started to play but Bonnie could not find her toys or her dolls. She looked where her sister's toys were usually kept. Her toys were not there. Next, she asked Mommy if her toys had moved during house cleaning time. Mommy told Bonnie that she had not moved any toys.

Bonnie went to her brothers' room and asked, "Have either of you seen my dolls and my doll buggy. Have you seen my other toys?"

"No," said Bobby.

Buster did not answer. He just looked away.

Bonnie went Mommy and said, "I think Buster hid my doll things and my other toys, too."

"Buster! Come here please!" said Mommy in a loud, firm voice.

Buster went right away when his mother called. He knew he had done something wrong, but he pretended otherwise and said, "Yes Mommy what do you want?"

She said, "Buster, did you do something with your sister's toys?"

Buster knew it was wrong to lie so he said, "Yes mother. I guess I was having a mean streak. I hid them and I will get everything for her. I know I was wrong, and I will ask her to forgive me."

Bonnie did forgive her brother and Buster learned that even if he has a bad day it is still wrong to do something bad to another.

And, that ends another story about Buster Bunny, who was not a regular rabbit because he lived in a city.

- 25 -
Riding Lessons

One summer I spent some time at a farm several miles away from Van Hook. I saw farming different from our neighbors the Olsons and learned how to ride a horse.

Farmer Johnson was always unshaven, grubby looking and usually grumpy. Mrs. Johnson reminded me of Mrs. Fitzpatrick – mostly because she was skinny and wore flour sack dresses. They had three daughters – one was just a baby.

They grew crops and had a few cows, chickens and pigs. Their garden always needed hoeing. That job fell to the oldest girl and me. I thought she was younger than me because she was considerably shorter than the girls my age in school. We didn't talk much. No one on the farm talked much.

The Johnsons had a team of work horses and two saddle horses. They had an old pickup truck but no car or tractor. All the field work was done with the work horses. Mrs. Johnson rode one of the saddle horses or walked when she took lunch out to the field for Mr. Johnson. She showed me some basics of cinching a saddle and mounting a horse from a wooden fence rail. She sent me to the field a few times after

I had practiced riding. I got comfortable riding at lope speed but never worked up the courage to try a gallop.

One day they left me alone and Johnson told me I could ride one of the horses while they were gone. I was firmly told that if the horse got sweaty, it would have to be wiped down before putting it back out to pasture. I was familiar with the procedure because Mrs. Johnson often galloped the horse into a sweat when she returned from the field. She showed me once and it became my chore.

I saw the family return and knew it was time to give up the ride. The towels were in the barn, so I rode in without dismounting. I remembered to duck my head going through the open door, but I didn't know that horses, at least the one I was on, didn't like to be ridden inside. Within feet of the door, the horse bucked, and my head was slammed against the underside of the haymow floor.

Johnson saw me get bucked off. Instead of yelling at me as I expected, he belly-laughed. He continued to chuckle as he wiped down the horse himself.

- 26 -
Riding a Young Bull

There was a small rodeo ring on the flats just west of Van Hook. In the late summer after I had been on Johnson's farm one of the men from town took me and several other boys to see a rodeo. There was no shade and the Nehi sodas we were given disappeared quickly. We filled the empty soda bottles with water from a small tank on the bed of a pickup truck.

The chutes were under the bleachers and we could smell the animals. The hot wind blew dust and the smell of animal waste into our faces from the corral on the other side of the rodeo ring.

About halfway through the program, the announcer invited us to participate in a young bull riding contest. Being bucked off the horse on the farm had tempered my confidence and I had no thought of volunteering. But, just by being there, we became volunteers and our host lined us up next to the chutes.

What I had seen when watching the men ride bulls and broncos made me think there must be some sort of craziness in the air. What sane person would volunteer to be pitched into the air and possibly stomped into pemmican by an animal ten times their weight?

111

They put a strap around the young bull's midsection, and we were supposed to wrap part of the strap around our hand to help our grip. When I got on, the calf took a few steps forward and shook a little. I thought it was going to continue that way until one of the rodeo men smacked the animal on the rump and tightened the cinch around its loins.

Immediately, things changed for the worse. I thought my arm was going to be pulled from the socket. It was a rule to use only one hand, but I tried to grab on with my other. Before I could reach the strap with my loose hand, my gripping hand slipped, and I was bucked into the air. I hit the ground hard!

I decided that we boys had been planned contributors to the entertainment of those who did a 'good' thing by taking us to the rodeo.

- 27 -
Cold as ...

North Dakota is famous or more likely infamous for bad, worse, and worst winters in memory. Many who grew up there have at least one story about how bad and cold the winter of (year of choice) was.

Rolvaag's novel *Giants in the Earth* tells about pioneer times and how the Hansa family copes with life in the Dakota Territory. Hansa's wife insists that he brave a storm to get a minister for a dying neighbor, but he gets stranded in the blizzard and dies alone on the unforgiving prairie.

My grandparents survived one of the worst winters in North Dakota's documented history; 1917-1918. My parents survived the winter of 1935-1936 when North Dakota's coldest temperature, -60, was recorded in February 1936, at Parshall, just ten miles from Van Hook. As you know I was born in October of '36.

With a few exceptions, because we didn't understand the seriousness of the situation, the winter of 1948-1949 in Van Hook was fun for kids. That was the winter of the mid-west hay lift when military C82 Flying Boxcars dropped hay to feed the starving cattle.

One time the snow drifted high enough to block the back door of our house and we had to use the front door. Another time we had to climb out a window and shovel the snow away from both doors. Many nights we couldn't see through the blowing snow to the light on the utility pole next to the road. During some of the stormy days we couldn't see the outhouse only a hundred feet towards town from the house. These were good enough indicators that it wasn't safe to send children to school.

Under normal bad weather conditions, someone in authority called the central telephone office and the operator[14] made an all-call on the party lines to let parents know about school closures. One day the blizzard stopped and there wasn't a cloud in the sky. Even early in the morning, looking outside was painful to the eyes. I was twelve and knew about snow blinding.

I'm sure widowed Grandma Marvel welcomed the clear, still day. She had been weather locked into a small three-bedroom house with seven children under the age of thirteen. Two of my younger school age brothers and I were summarily pushed out the door with scarves over our faces and our lunches in mittened hands.

We got to the school and found it closed. I read the note on the door, "Pipes frozen – closed until further notice." There had not been a call from telephone central – that winter many phone lines were compromised by snow that had drifted onto the wires.

---

[14] Grandmother Josine Benson.

We returned home and I saw that Grandma Marvel had managed to get enough of the hard-packed snow away from the outhouse door so a boy and a bucket would fit through. Among other things, we hadn't been able to get to the outhouse, so we filled buckets in the cellar. I was the oldest boy, so guess what! And, she didn't have to tell me to close the door and latch it when I was through dumping the pails of waste. I remember one time earlier in the winter (or it could have been the winter before) when the outhouse door blew open and the snow filled it up to the seats. I had to shovel it out.

A news broadcast that night told us that the temperature in some parts of west-central North Dakota had been -53 degrees the previous night.

I heard a story that outhouses in towns were always placed towards the town so if someone missed it in a winter storm, they would end up in town instead of on the open prairie like Per Hansa. Our house was at the edge of town and our farmer neighbor loaned us a rope to tie from our back porch to the outhouse so we could guide ourselves back and forth in the dark. He told us that having the rope was also a good idea in case of the arrival of a sudden blizzard while someone was indisposed away from the house.

All of the roads and even the railroad had been closed for some time so there was no way in or out of town except by horse and sled. Nearly every local farmer had both but not many in town were so equipped. It wouldn't have made much difference anyway; the nearest 'store bought' supplies were probably in Minot about 70 miles away.

I remember hearing that some of the townsmen borrowed a horse and sled to get what was left of the coal in the abandoned lignite mine (our cave) just outside of town. Lignite is the lowest of coal grades, so people didn't use it because more of it turned into clinkers than heat. However, when the good stuff ran out, it turned out to be a suitable substitute for no fuel at all.

On a day when the wind wasn't blowing, my brother and I took a grocery list to the store. The store shelves were nearly empty and had none of the items on Grandma Marvel's list. We did have home canned vegetables and our farmer neighbor kept us in eggs and milk. We made butter for our homemade bread by whipping the cream that rose to the top of the raw milk.

That winter, Van Hook, North Dakota, was snowed in for over thirty days.

– 28 –
On Ice with no Skates

*H*ans Brinker and the Silver Skates was required reading for fifth graders in Van Hook schools. The story is about a poor boy in Holland who is a good skater but only has wooden skates.

Someone in Van Hook pushed snow into a large rectangle and put in enough water to make a skating rink. Neither Michael Fitzpatrick nor I had skates. We thought of our shoes as wooden skates and figured we could learn to skate on them. We watched kids who had boot or clamp-on skates to learn the motions. It was hard to get a grip on the ice with flat shoes, but we tried. We did manage to make ourselves move but not very gracefully.

Michael and I decided to just run and slide after a number of attempts at shoe skating. I got myself going faster by running on the snow at the edge of the rink so I could slide farther. It worked great and soon Michael and I were competing to slide the farthest.

I needed to be home at dusk and Michael was sure to be on the brink of being in trouble with his mom again, so we decided to take our last run and slide for the win. Michael went first and slid farther than he or I had before. I got a good run along the bank and used the resting bench as a springboard for greater acceleration. I was in the air a good distance before I hit the ice.

The instant I was in the air I knew I was going to win – my feet were flying. But I had no control in the air and even less once my feet hit the ice. My feet slid fast, but gravity took over and – crack – I landed on the back of my head. It hurt as much or even more than when I got beaned with the baseball.

Grandma Marvel told me when I was older that I was awake but quite confused when one of the men brought me home. She told me that she had kept me home from school for three days and the weekend because I was sick and 'out of it'. All I remember is the nearly continuous dizziness and regurgitation.

I probably had a serious concussion but, in those days, kids only went to the doctor if their 'arm was cut off'.

The next winter I had a pair of used clamp-on skates that were designed to fit on boots or very sturdy shoes. The first time I tried to put them on over my overshoes the clamps cut through the rubber. The overshoes leaked the rest of the winter.

Perhaps wooden skates wouldn't have been so bad after all.

- 29 -
Shadow Boxer

A group of men started a youth boxing club to keep boys in Van Hook busy during the cold winter evenings and weekends. They assembled pre-teen boys over age six at the fire station on Saturday mornings and sometimes on Wednesdays[15] after school for training in the manly art of self-defense.

Uncle Lowell and I walked the half mile from our house unless there was a blizzard. Regular snow wasn't a problem – we just followed the light from pole to pole. Even if widowed Grandma Marvel wanted to drive her 1939 Mercury on winter days, it probably would have taken as long to warm it up as it did for us to walk to or from the fire station.

The two oil heaters kept the station hot so even stripped to our shorts we seldom had goose bumps on our pasty skin. I didn't have trunks of my own, so I usually chose a pair from those that hung on the lower row of hooks along the wall where the volunteer fireman's gear was stowed. There were no shorts small enough for me, so I had to cinch them

[15] In the 1940s and even the 1950s students in fourth grade and above were released from school an hour early on Wednesdays to attend catechism classes. Those who didn't attend a church just went home.

up with a string or tuck them into the waist band of my Jockeys.

Even if it was cold inside, a shirt of any kind wasn't a part of the boxing uniform. The fire station, like most places, didn't have inside toilets so we stripped to our underwear and put on our boxing shorts in public. That wasn't a real problem for even the most modest of us. Women or girls were never there.

Some dads and a few other men were involved as trainers. One of the men talked about seeing my older cousin Arne Laird fight in Golden Gloves matches and told about an unusual punch he used. It was an overhead sweep ending with the glove sliding down the opponent's nose. Cousin Arne seemed to be some kind of a hero because he also boxed welterweight in the Army.

Some man came to our house after supper on Friday or Saturday evenings (sometimes both) and took Uncle Lowell and me along with a carload of other boys to matches at the station. One time I was included in a trip to Parshall, ten miles away, to fight the kids there.

Volunteer firemen moved the fire trucks and trailers outside on competition nights. They set up a ring surrounded by folding chairs in the middle of the concrete floor. Matches were just like practices in one respect – there were never girls or women there.

We were paired by weight. I was short but weighed about the same as boys much taller. Everyone there was thin. In fact, I don't remember ever seeing a kid who wasn't skinny in Van Hook. I cannot imagine and certainly don't remember how they found anyone as small as Uncle Lowell for his match. I'm not sure he even had a fight.

We usually fought three rounds. I remember the gloves being so big that even in practice on the big bag my pencil thin arms got tired almost immediately. My taking a full swing was almost impossible after the second round. I did try to use my cousin's punch, but it was ineffective. When and if I could get the glove moving the wind past the face of an opponent only served to cool his perspiring body.

I didn't score enough points on an opponent to even rate a draw during my first few matches. In fact, I don't remember if I hit any one of the long armed taller boys with whom I was matched by weight. Their best defense was to hold one glove on my head so I could only swing under their arm or try to knock their arm to the side and try to move in. Then there was always their other long arm being used for hitting me. I don't think I took any real hard hits either. The gloves were probably just as heavy on long arms – maybe heavier.

One Saturday evening I was up, and immediately into the first round my taller opponent was beating the tar out of me. Donald Ranum (or maybe it was his brother Keith) as I remember was the best in my weight class and I had not been up against him before. He not only held me off with his long arms but was able to haymaker me several times. None of

121

the hits was more than my hard head and stubborn disposition could take, but they did get my attention. It was occurring to me that perhaps boxing was something for which I wasn't even remotely well suited.

During the second or maybe the third round as his hammering on me continued, I realized that, like it had been at the rodeo, participating in that fine art of self-defense may not have been for the benefit of us boys at all. The Ranums and Michael Fitzpatrick seemed to really enjoy themselves. They, of course, had not lost a match or had a draw except when they fought each other.

One of the men laughed loudly when Ranum laid a haymaker on the side of my head spinning me to the ropes. During the mandatory eight-count by the referee, it also hit me that the men were cheering, smoking, and drinking tavern smelling coffee from thermoses. They were having a good time and the boxing boys in the ring were there for their enjoyment.

Participating in the keep-the-boys-busy program was even more frustrating after realizing the purpose of our being involved. I wanted to quit but it would have been far better to have my nose broken than being called a quitter.

Sometimes we boys listened to the professional prize fights on the radio at the fire station with the men. The men talked about the boxing future of some of the boys in the club. My name never came up as having any potential. I still remember one saying something like, "Benson could only score if he was boxing his own shadow and maybe not even then."

Those events, I guess, were man – boy bonding events. Grandma Marvel must have thought that since we had little adult male influence, the boxing club would be a good thing for us.

However, I always thought of the activities as "Morris takes another pounding" events.

- 30 -
Spontaneous Combustion

The coal furnace and coal bin were in the dirt floor cellar of the Wilber house. Every winter morning, I took the still warm, sometimes still glowing clinkers from the furnace fire pit with tongs and put them on the floor against the cellar wall. I was also responsible for taking the clinkers to a pile near the outhouse after they cooled. We kept the ashes in a separate pile to be put on the snow for a non-slip path to the road and to the outhouse.

Sometimes, I would take a small still glowing clinker with the tongs, run up the stairs and pitch it into the snow to see how far down it would sink before it got too cool to melt the snow.

The steam from hot clinkers or ashes on snow has a smell I have not forgotten. It is similar to rain splashing on recently burned prairie grass.

One night the fire went out and it took me nearly an hour to ignite the lignite coal with pages from an outdated catalog soaked in kerosene. We didn't have kindling wood. I came up with what I thought was a clever idea based on some flawed observations made during my fire building experiences. Later that winter the night fire went out again and I initiated my idea.

Small, thin pieces of coal started easier than larger pieces, even if the larger pieces had thin edges. My inexperience logic was: if small chips ignited quicker than chunks, the fine coal dust would start even faster. I soaked some small chips and catalog pages with kerosene and started a small fire with some glowing clinker shards on the bottom of the firebox.

I sorted the coal residue on the floor into separate piles of dust and chips. My plan was to put coal dust on the starting fire to make it hotter and have a scoop of small chips ready to put on top of the burning coal dust. I scooped about a fourth of a shovel full of dust thinking that more than that might smother the "starter chips" in the firebox.

I pitched the dust into the firebox and turned to scoop up the chips.

Kaboom! I landed face first in the coal bin with a terrible ringing in my ears. I must have been propelled into the coal bin wall too. Several jars of vegetables were knocked off the shelves and broken.

Grandma Marvel came running down but decided I wasn't hurt except for singed hair on the back of my head. She went back upstairs because the other six kids had been awakened by the sound. I still had to start the fire and clean up the broken jars and vegetable mess.

Years later I learned about grain elevator and sawmill dust explosions. Then, I understood what had happened.

Combustible dust of any kind with a heat source is very volatile.

- 31 -
Stick Fight

Grandma Marvel wasn't home for some reason one winter evening and she'd left 12-year-old me in charge!

I took the stick out of the lower end of a window shade for a reason only a twelve-year-old would have. I swished the stick around in the air as if to fight some imaginary foe. I took a few swipes at Uncle Lowell and he went off somewhere to read. Uncle David became my next target. He wasn't happy being the object of my thrusts even though I never actually touched him. Aunt Connie, Aunt Beth, Uncle Arne, and Uncle Ronald were too little to be targets or perhaps they were already in bed for the night. That part I don't remember.

Uncle David left for a while but when he returned, I started the thrusting and imaginary parrying again. He struck back.

I didn't know that he had gone to get a weapon of his own. It was a jar of Vicks VapoRub. I was in a superior position on the arm of our couch, but he fired the jar at me from close range. I don't think he aimed for my head, but the jar struck me hard enough to draw blood just above my eye. I don't remember which eye it was, but I remember the bleeding. It was a mess.

Grandma Marvel arrived home about the same time as I was starting to clean up blood on the floor and kitchen sink. It came off the linoleum in the kitchen OK, but she had to use some bleach to take the spots off the wood floor in the living room. It was probably a good thing for my wellbeing that it didn't splatter on the couch or any of her doilies.

I'm not sure what my punishment was but I never attacked Uncle David again. Even when he was little, he stood up for himself.

- 32 -
Trailblazer

Someone gave us two new sleds one Christmas in Van Hook. The Trailblazer was long enough for Uncle Lowell, Uncle David and me to sit on. Aunts Connie and Beth could ride on the smaller Flexible Flyer if Grandma Marvel could get Uncle Lowell or me to pull them. Our old sled was one that had been repainted and given to us as a gift when winter set in the year before. It had nice paint but the flexing crack in the center board pinched the user.

Uncle Arne and Uncle Ronald were too small to be out in freezing weather and the girls didn't go out very often. Only Uncle Lowell and I were allowed outside most of the time; but there were times when we had to take Uncle David with us. We had the Flexible Flyer, the Trailblazer and the hand-me-down. Uncle Lowell and I worked out a take turns system for the Trailblazer, but Uncle David seldom got a turn on one of the new sleds.

We removed the paint from the new sled's runners by belly flopping on the gravel road and waxed the runners with Grandma Marvel's canning paraffin. Belly flopping on the hand-me-down to remove last year's rust was dangerous because the rivets were loose, and the runners would lean to one side or the other. We pulled Uncle David on it to scrape off the rust.

We usually went sledding where the road had been cut through an ancient riverbank just a few hundred yards outside of town. The drifting snow had filled the cut, so the original shape of the bluff was restored. And, it formed a cornice on which we dared each other to slide. It was wind packed so well that it didn't break even when the older boys took our Trailblazer to test their mettle.

One of our favorite sledding places was on the road near what we called the cliffs just to the west of town. The road to Sanish cut downhill through an ancient riverbank and its surface was usually firmly packed but rutted. The trick to go fastest and farthest was to straddle a rut to the bottom of the hill.

The Trailblazer was popular with other boys too. Most of them just asked for a turn on it but now and then an older boy would extend his turn. Boys using the Trailblazer usually won the distance contest. Sometimes it would be passed from older boy to older boy many times before we got it back. Uncle Lowell and I didn't have permission to slide there but, if we wanted our borrowed Trailblazer back, that was where we would have to go.

It was a thrill to slide along a cornice edge knowing that the snow was unsupported by anything except its frozen self. Some of the older boys used our fast turning Trailblazer to slide directly toward the edge and make a quick turn to be parallel with it. I never saw anyone go straight off the edge or tumble down after turning. The winner was the one who could go the closest to the edge without going over. It wasn't quite as dangerous as first perceived; the drop after a cornice collapse was only about six or eight feet into soft snow below. That was about the same as doing a flip off the outhouse into the snowbank below.

Uncles Arnie and Ronald got to sledding age in Alexandria, MN, and the Trailblazer became theirs.

- 33 -
Bicycle Lessons

U ncle Lowell and I got a good used bicycle to share at Christmas, 1947 or 1948. When springtime came, like with the Trailblazer sled, we worked out a system of sharing. But we didn't have to share with Uncle David.

It didn't have fenders, but Grandma Marvel found some that fit. She also found a rack that fit over the rear wheel so Lowell and I thought we could use it for the back seat and ride together. It was too flimsy for that, but it did work fairly well for tying on a few groceries.

I wasn't much bigger than Lowell, but I was a little stronger so when we doubled, I got the seat but had to peddle with him sideways on the top tube of the frame. That was difficult but it worked.

One day we discovered that he could balance on the handlebars and put one or both feet lightly on the front fender for stabilization. It was harder for me to steer but easier for me to peddle. Soon after learning those skills we decided to test our ability to go fast.

We thought about riding down the hill on the road going towards Sanish but there was too much loose gravel. Our other option was to take the dirt trail down the hill to the railroad tracks.

We were going faster than either of us imagined we could go when we hit a small bump. The jolt was enough to separate Uncle Lowell's foot from the fender. When he adjusted, his heel went into the spokes behind the fork.

The stop was as if we hit a wall. Uncle Lowell was thrown to the trail and I was catapulted over him. Once again, Grandma Marvel had wounded boys. Uncle Lowell had a nasty cut on his heel, and I had another scrape on my head.

Right! Neither of us was wearing shoes. And, that was long before bicycle helmets were available.

One of the Ranum boys clipped a playing card to the frame of his bicycle so the flipping on the spokes made it sound like a motorcycle engine. I did the same.

Motorcycles had to be raced. Ranum and I raced on the flat road and won about the same number of times. One day we decided to race downhill. We started at the top end of the Olson brothers' road that ran past our house to the west. It was fairly smooth and promised a good fast race.

It was lunch time and Ranum decided to take one last run. I was adjusting the card on my spokes and he took off. He would win with what I thought was an unfair start, so I instinctively took a shortcut.

I went down the hill across the field toward our house. I would cut him off just after the curve at the end of Olson's road where it joined the main road. I hadn't thought about Grandma Marvel's clotheslines being in my shortcut path. I was going nearly as fast as I had ever gone on the flat road. I saw the first line and ducked. I wasn't low enough for the sagging forth line. It caught me just above the eyes. The bike kept going and I landed and skidded on my back.

Any time someone makes a comment about someone being clothes lined in a football game, I remember my real clotheslining.

- 34 -
Prince

Prince was our dog in Van Hook. One of our neighbor's dogs had a litter and we got him after he was weaned the spring of 1947. He was mix-breed but looked and acted like a sheep dog. He was mostly black but had a few white spots.

Most people fed their dog table scraps. Grandma Marvel made soup with ham bones but after the flavor was cooked out, he would get the bone (Just like Jiggs when we had him). If we had beef roast or pork chops with bones, he got them. Now and then he'd follow me to Grendahl's store. Well, I didn't discourage him because I could get a free fresh bone for him. Sometimes Grandma Marvel and other ladies would ask for a dog bone, but the butcher knew who would be having soup for dinner.

Prince, like most dogs of his day, wasn't a house dog. In the summer he slept anywhere he wanted to but always outside. Grandma Marvel and I made a lean-to with scrap boards on the rail of the back porch for him to sleep in the winter. She put an old blanket on the lean-to floor and tacked an old blanket to the top and side away from the house for insulation. I had to dig snow away from his lean-to a few times so he could get out. Well, I'm sure he could have on his own but just didn't need to.

We imagined him to be a sled dog and tried to get him to pull the Trailblazer. He saw his role differently. He just sat in front of the sled or tried to climb on it with us. He wouldn't even pull it empty for me.

Lowell and I tried to get him to pull the Radio Flyer to pull water home from the town pump. That didn't work either.

He was nearly always with me when I was playing ball, cowboys and Indians, or when some of us would sneak off to the cave or try swimming in the alkali pond outside of town.

We were sad because there wasn't room for him in our car or Uncle Elmo's truck to take him along when we moved to Minnesota. Our neighbor Goff Olson said he would try to take care of him.

I had wondered where we left Jiggs or where he left us, but I know about Prince.

- 35 -
Radiation

The Wilber house where we lived in Van Hook was still not fully insulated during the winter of 1948-49 and was rarely warm. Grandma Marvel blamed that for my having several colds and ear infections.

I don't remember listening to a Minot radio station, but I do remember WCCO Minneapolis and KFYR Bismarck. Every evening one or the other would have *Jack Armstrong the All-American Boy*, *The Green Hornet*, *The Shadow*, *Captain Midnight*, and other shows designed to stir the imagination of boys my age. (And just like now, convince boys to bug their parents for advertised products.)

But I became a speaker hog. I couldn't hear without being close or having the radio at full blast. My hearing became worse and my throat was sore nearly all the time.

Dr. Blatherwick, son of the doctor who had delivered me in Sanish, held appointments in Van Hook only once a week. Colds or earaches were not considered a real reason to spend money on a doctor visit. Vicks VapoRub on the chest or under the nose for the cold and a warm cloth on the affected ear was usually good enough. When my speaker hogging became an issue, Grandma Marvel did get me in to see him.

He told her I would have to have my tonsils and adenoids removed but would have to go to Minot to have the operations. He only did emergency surgery if someone had to have a wound or injury sewn up.

In Minot, Dr. Ayash[16] wasn't able to get all of the adenoids by surgery because they had grown into my inner ear channels. I'm not sure how many post-surgery visits I had with him but it must have been on the third or fourth when I realized that there was something different about the procedure he was using. With that realization, treatment became unnerving to me.

He would come into the room wearing what appeared to be a very heavy lab coat. A nurse, also wearing a heavy lab outfit, brought a large cylinder that she seemed to have some difficulty carrying. I was covered with a heavy blanket and Grandma Marvel wasn't allowed in the room. Dr. Ayash put on gloves that went all the way up to the sleeves of his coat. He took what looked like a small silver cylinder, rounded on each end, on the end of a piece of piano wire out of the heavy container.

That thing was greased with something the consistency of Vaseline and smelled like mint. He put the silver thing up my nose one nostril at a time. When I asked about the blanket, lab coats and case for the object I learned that they were lead and the lead was to protect me from radiation.

---

[16] Mother always made a point of identifying him as an Iranian.

I knew what most eleven or twelve-year-old boys knew about radiation. When we had lived in Pasco, WA, during the WWII years, I had overheard one of the women say that people who worked at the Hanford Atomic Energy Pant would turn green from the radiation.

When he came into the room on what may have been my last visit and before he took the "wire" out of the lead case, I said that I had to go to the toilet. It had occurred to me that my brain wasn't protected from whatever it was he was putting up my nose. I found a restroom on another floor and crawled onto a ledge behind some equipment. They found me but I don't remember what happened after that.

He was using radium to burn the adenoid tissue from my inner ear. Now and then I worry about my brain and pituitary gland having been seriously affected by the radium treatment. I'm 82 at the time of this writing and unlike many others, I've suffered no ill effects from the procedures.[17]

---

[17] During the 1940s, '50s and '60s, tens of thousands – children, mostly – received a treatment called nasal radium therapy, in which a radium-tipped probe was inserted in the nostrils. At the time the procedure, pioneered by doctors at Johns Hopkins, looked like a successful way to treat hearing loss, tonsillitis and colds. Today, it appears to have been a serious mistake.

- 36 -
Transition

Uncle Ronald was just a month from being three and it was nearly half a year before I'd be thirteen when we left North Dakota after school was out in 1949.

Grandma Marvel's brother Elmo drove up from Minnesota with his grain truck to haul whatever household things we had. Grandma Marvel was legally blind, but she drove our 1939 Mercury to Minnesota.

We stayed with Grandpa and Grandma Larson or with Uncle Elmo and his wife Aunt Laura on their farms near Kensington.

Summer, 1949, at Grandpa Larson's farm.
David, Lowell, Me, Mother
Arne, Connie, Beth Ronald

Grandpa taught me two things I still remember. At the right of the picture you see the foundation laid for a future addition to their house. Grandma had grass planted there. I cannot remember mowing grass until I was allowed, well given, that task. It was logical to me to push the reel mower in one direction and push it back next to what I had cut. Grandpa showed me that going one way distributed the grass onto the yet uncut. He told me when I came back on that row, I would be cutting the grass twice.

He also showed me that even a twelve-year-old boy could lift nearly a ton of hay into the haymow of the barn with a pully system.

I don't remember how long we stayed there until Grandma Marvel found a place near Holmes City. It was a farmhouse on a small hill a short walk to the Oscar Lake home of a family named Kemppinen. The family of Finns had a sauna and I learned that steaming up and running into a snowbank or cold lake in full sweat. Until I tried it I thought they were crazy, but that's what they did.

Mr. Kemppinen taught me how to put a worm on a hook. The training came to fruition when I caught a Blue Gill Sunfish larger than he had seen in his many years of fishing. It weighed 1 lb. 8 oz. on his fishing scale. He suggested I take it into Alexandria and enter it in the Cowing Robards

Sporting Goods fish contest. I anticipated the top prize – a rod and reel.

Grandma Marvel couldn't get into Alex that day, so we put the fish in the refrigerator overnight and took it the next day. The fish lost weight and was only 1 lb. 6 oz. at the store. It was on display for a week and was at first place until the last day of the weekly contest. Someone brought in a Blue Gill weighing 1 lb. 7 oz. and I took second place. The prize was a pack of hooks and roll of fishing line.

The Oliver and Muriel Omland farm was nearby too. One of the first kids I met was their son LeRoy. I'm sure he knew his parents were supplying milk and eggs to the widow with seven kids, but he never said anything to me.[18]

Another kid I met was a little older. I believe his last name was Johnson, but I can't remember his first. I was impressed that he had a Remington pump action .22 rifle. He loaned me his single shot .22 and took me squirrel shooting. At times we shot enough to supply dinner for both families.

The Johnson family had Monopoly marathons and I was invited one time (or maybe more). One event lasted until early morning and I walked home in the moonlight. Every

---

[18]We did talk about it in high school and he said something like, "that's just the way my parents are."

tree shadow on the road became some kind of monster even though I knew better.

That summer Uncle Elmo taught me how to shoot a 10-gauge shotgun. I had already shot Johnson's .22 enough to think I knew how. He explained that the shotgun would kick more than any .22. He explained that I shouldn't push the butt into my shoulder because it would knock me over. He was right; it kicked and kicked hard.

After he finished laughing, he explained it had to be held tight to the shoulder to prevent getting bruised. It still knocked me back a little when I fired the next shell. Uncle Elmo was a nice man, but he was mischievous too.

That fall, all of us except Uncle Arne and Uncle Ronald started school in Holmes City.

- 37 -
Swimming Lesson

Dog paddling in the little alkali pond near Van Hook, ND, was my first attempt at swimming after my horse trough experience at one of the Washington orchards. Since our time next to the Missouri River, Grandma Marvel had always cautioned us about water (me especially) when we camped near a river or pond, so I was a little leery of water deeper than my waist. And the bayou cautions about snakes and gators had not yet left my mind.

Kemppinens had a dock and I could walk at the edge into water up to my arm pits. But I always held on to the dock on the way out. I would step a little to the side and splash my way to the shore. I watched the Kemppinens dive off the end of the dock and swim to the reed patch and back.

The older Kemppinen girl who was also our babysitter at times said she would hold me up so I could practice but I never went beyond the end of the dock. Heeding Grandma Marvel's cautions, where I couldn't see the bottom, I didn't go.

I met some older boys from school to go fishing, I thought. One said they needed bait and some new hooks, so we rode our bikes about three miles into Holmes City. One of the boys asked me if I could swim. To which I probably replied in the negative. At least one of them knew I could dog paddle because he was at Kemppinen's dock a few times when I was doing my fearful attempts.

They took another boy and me by boat to a floating raft on Grant Lake and left us there. They said they would chum the water as they rowed to shore so we could catch a few fish from the raft. And, they did throw bait into the water as they rowed to the dock.

After a while, I'm not sure how long, the boy with me on the raft told me they weren't coming back, and we would have to swim to the dock. I immediately looked into the water to see if I could see the bottom. I couldn't. He dove in, swam to the dock and disappeared. I was alone on the raft with two fishing poles and a can with two minnows.

I yelled as loud as I could in my squeaky, prepubescent voice that I couldn't swim. Eventually, I decided they were going to leave me there for the night so I eased my way into the water and shoved as hard as I could against the raft with my feet and dog paddled the rest of the way to the dock.

When I got ashore, I heard the shout, "Hey Benson, I thought you said you couldn't swim."

They were hiding and waiting for me to make it to shore on my own. They had a plan. I figured later that it was sort of like taking someone snipe hunting but on the water.

Their trick significantly reduced my fear of deep water and I eventually became a good swimmer.

Postscript

Greetings of the Season
and best wishes for your
happiness

The Christmas of 1949 we got a card and note from Goff and Hub.

He wrote:

Dear Morris;

Your dog Prince was a very nice looking dog the last time I saw him lost. He was a bum around town. Guess he missed you and the kids too much to make friends with grownups. I yelled at him a lot when he was a pup so he couldn't get in the habit of following me instead of you. I could easily have stolen the dog from you then. He remembered me – and not very favorably either.

When I tried to coax him to stick around after you had to leave him here. He would wag his tail but he never let me pet him although he came over and sniffed of me every time I was on foot.

He came up here every day for about a month and looked for you kids at the Wilber house and up to my house but he finally quit coming. I had feed set out for him and he ate it but always left as soon as he saw or heard me.

I'm sorry he didn't trust me but I blame myself 'cause I always growled at him. Don't think for a moment I didn't like him. He was a swell dog and I'd have given him a place to sleep and enough to eat, only, I couldn't make him understand.

How is the boxing business in Minn.? Are you fellows holding your own? Hope you like your new friends and new home.

If you come out this way, stop in and say hello anyhow.

PS: I'm putting a couple of Bucks in for Christmas and your Birthday.

Sincerely,

Goff

--- end ---

We moved 10 miles from Holmes City, MN, to Alexandria, MN, in the spring of 1950.

About the Author

John Morris Benson was born in Sanish, ND, in 1936. In the late 1940s, his widowed mother moved with her seven children from Van Hook, ND, to Alexandria, MN. He was graduated from Central High School in 1955.

His nearly ten-year Cold War military service was with the Army Security Agency. He served in the U.S., Far East, and Europe.

Benson earned his BA in Education from Central Washington University. While teaching in Kelso, WA, he earned his MS in School Administration at Portland State University.

He and his wife since 1959 live in Vancouver, WA. They have three adult children, seven adult grandchildren, a great-grandson, and a great granddaughter.

Benson's first writing was classified electronic equipment documentation for the Army Security Agency. While teaching, several of his vocational education articles were published in national journals.

His 2012 novel, *An Odyssey of Illusions,* was a 2013 Eric Hoffer Award finalist. In 2017 his 'as told to me' "I'm a Blessed Man" was published by Gospel Publishing House's "Live" weekly journal. Benson self-published *Nescient Decoy* and *Echoes of Nam.* He contributed to *Chicken Soup for the Soul: The Best Advice I Ever Heard.*

www.ingramcontent.com/pod-product-compliance
Lightning Source LLC
Chambersburg PA
CBHW060459280326
41933CB00014B/2792